UNIVERSAL BROTHERHOOD:

Quranic solutions to overcome racism and oppression

JIHAD A RASUWL

Copyright © 2012. Jihad A Rasuwl
All rights reserved.

ISBN: 098513660X
ISBN-13: 9780985136604

CONTENTS

About the Author v
Preface xi
Chapter 1 1
Chapter 2 23
Chapter 3 45
Chapter 4 67
Chapter 5 79
Chapter 6 87
Chapter 7 109
Chapter 8 111
Chapter 9 123
Chapter 10 131
Chapter 11 137
Chapter 12 143
Chapter 13 153
Chapter 14 163
Index 173
Notes 179

ABOUT THE AUTHOR

I was born in Allentown, Pennsylvania in 1972. I grew up in South Jamaica Queens during the seventies and eighties. My elementary school, P.S. 223 was all black, just like the neighborhood we lived in. All the families on my block were African American on 142nd Street in South Jamaica, except for my Jamaican neighbor, Ms. Florence. My neighbors were either first or second generation New Yorkers that migrated from the South to get away from racism and oppression. It was ironic considering that New York was just as segregated as Birmingham, Alabama. There was only one elderly man around the corner from us that was white. Besides him, the only other whites that I saw in my neighborhood were school teachers, the firemen in the firehouse on Rockaway Boulevard, the guys who climbed the telephone poles, and the police.

By junior high school we were bused into an Italian neighborhood in Howard Beach. There were several incidents where blacks were chased out of that neighborhood and beaten just for being black which resulted in death. I can remember the white parents yelling, "Go back to your own neighborhood, niggers!" as the other black eighth graders and myself watched from inside the school bus with a million questions whirling around in our minds.

I had a Christian mother that took me to church three times a week. She claimed that I needed to read the Bible to be a better person. I remembered seeing crosses around the necks of the racist people in the Italian neighborhood that I went to school in, not to mention the Bible reading Christians that burned crosses on the land of the blacks that were ran out of the South. I was convinced that there was a connection between the Bible and racism.

Universal Brotherhood: Quranic solutions to overcome racism and oppression

Later on in life I attended Norfolk State University and the University of Minnesota where I studied Ancient Near Eastern Studies to get a better understanding of the Bible. It was interesting; however, about half way through my studies I began to realize the ineffectiveness of higher education in terms of solving the social problems for the common man. Most college graduates can tell you where to put the semicolon and where to start a new paragraph, but they can't show you how to go down to the hood and improve the lives of the common people. Everyone I met was so into obtaining credentials to begin a career until they were so distanced from the average person that they often did more criticizing than helping.

Secondly, the hypocrisy of the "objective" approach was something else that I had a problem with. The truth is that the second a man takes a position on any subject, all objectivity is lost. Does the media give someone the government declares an enemy the same amount of time to defend himself as they do criticizing him? However, as writers, we are supposed to be so neutral in our works until it's hard to often see where we are going with our ideas or where we stand. We are supposed to play the middle so hard until much work is finished without even saying what needs to be said, or without even proposing any effective solutions out of fear of being "biased".

The only way that I saw that I could make any effective change in society is to work independently without having to depend on the censorship of wealthy sponsors who have their own political objectives that are in contrast to what I believe is the truth. If I have to worry about writing what the University President or the head of my department wants to hear to save my position as a professor then I might as well not write anything, or pursue my objective outside of the "academic" world.

The idea to write this book came to me in 2001. I picked it up here and there, but the drive wasn't there. One chilly morning I was riding down Highway 90 in North Florida on my way home from work in 2009. A deputy from the Sherriff's department put his siren on and pulled me over for wearing headphones. The white officer came up to my passenger's side window. His first words were, "Yeah, I saw you leaning back 'pimping' with your headphones on…"

From that point I knew where the traffic stop was going. I've been through the racial profiling routine so many times until I've learned to keep a JVC video recorder with me just for these types of incidents. The

About the Author

officer went back to his car and ran my license. By the time he came back I had my JVC recording everything. He told me to step out of the car. He then said that if I didn't let him search the car for drugs that he was going to take me to jail, or have me stand on the side of the road for a few hours (in the cold in my t-shirt).

I had several appointments that morning, so I told him to just search the car. After a few minutes he realized that he was being recorded. He picked up the recorder and pointed it at me. He asked me, "Do you want it on me or on you?!"

I told him to put it right back where it was at. Instead, he turned it off. Afterwards, he gave me a ticket for not only the headphones, but for not having my current address on my license and for not maintaining my lane. How a man can pull over without crossing the bicycle lane is a mystery to me. His exact words were, "I'm giving you these tickets because I don't like your attitude." I never knew that there was an attitude ticket either. The traffic stop resulted in four hundred dollars in tickets.

For two months until I reached traffic court I thought about numerous instances when I was charged for crimes that I didn't commit by white police officers, not to mention employment discrimination, and other situations. Some days it was real hard for my anger not to overcome me where I would take it out on one of my friends. It was almost impossible for me to smile, because I didn't know where the next attack would come from.

In court there were about ten officers from the City of Madison Police Department, the Madison County Sherriff's Department, and the Florida State Police Highway Patrol. Although Madison County is about fifty percent African American and fifty percent Caucasian all of the officers were white males, including the judge. I sat and listened to over two dozen traffic cases for close to three hours. People presented their cases, some of them with lawyers, trying to have their tickets thrown out. The judge rarely lifted his head up to even look at them or to pay attention to what they had to say.

I sat in the long wooden pew rehearsing over and over what I would say as I looked out the giant windows that were large enough to sit a Cadillac in upright. There was a dismal silence as each defendant waited patiently to have their presentation body slammed. I felt like an ant watching an elephant falling towards it, caught in between choosing a strategy or acceptance of the inevitable loss to come. Me being properly groomed, wearing a suit and tie, with all of my case law and notes organized on a clip board, didn't relax me either.

Finally my name was called and the deputy presented his side of the case: wearing the headphones, "swerving" over the bicycle lane, and having the worse attitude that he had ever saw in his life. Each word made me relive the humiliation he put me through. Finally when it was my turn, I said, "Despite what the deputy has said I have evidence that his allegations are false, and I have recorded the traffic stop to prove that this is a typical case of racial profiling…" From that point I pulled out a copy of the DVD and lifted it up in the air. For the first time I saw the judge lift up his face and pay attention to what a defendant (myself) had to say.

I showed that the officer had mal intent and a lack of professionalism by writing the tickets up as moving violations where they were non-moving, so that I could pay double the amount in fines. Then I showed that I would have to cross the bicycle lane in order to pull over. The judge threw out the "failing to maintain a lane ticket" and reduced the headphone ticket to a non-moving violation. I ended up only paying one hundred dollars instead of four hundred.

I left the courtroom that day reflecting on how I was the only one out of over two dozen people that had his car searched for drugs and humiliated during a routine traffic stop, but also the only one that beat a ticket, paying just a quarter the amount of the initial tickets.

It showed me two things: racism and oppression is real, and that there is hope and optimism to overcome it no matter what level it's on. There were many white people in court that shared the same anger that I did. Although they weren't searched for drugs, they were, nonetheless, victims of a system that squeezes money out of the poor in times of recession through frivolous tickets and taxes. Although I was comfortable with life and fortunate to be employed during a time of a recession, I almost forgot the realities that many of us face as being poor people. However, experience taught me to be a leader. I monitor the police and learn case law. I travel with a camcorder to make sure that there is no ambiguity in court when someone wants to lie against me. Unlike voice recordings, video recordings are admissible in court in most cases. I've learned to master the law to make the authorities serve my needs, as their "serve and protect" motto suggests, instead of vice versa.

I knew that the only reason that society continues to exploit people the way it does is because most people don't understand how a Judeo-Christian society operates, especially towards those of African descent. Secondly, they don't have a clue on how to solve any of the injustices that exist in a strategic way. I'm convinced that if I could explain in detail of not only the Judeo-Christian world's position towards racism and oppression, but to offer Quranic solutions, then, not only could I help others improve their living conditions, but we could collectively change society, and I, as an individual, would not have to confront the same injustices over and over repeatedly.

PREFACE

This work was sparked off by a conversation between two of my friends when I was living in Norfolk, Virginia. Akeel, an African American Muslim from Atlanta, Georgia asked his friend, Mathew, from Newport News, Virginia how he could follow Christianity, considering that Christians were responsible for the enslavement and persecution of Blacks. Mathew's response was, "The Arab's had slaves, too." Akeel sat silently not knowing what to say. Mathew put a knife in Akeel's idea and killed every rehearsed line that he had in his mind.

It's true that *people*, regardless of religious denomination, do wrong, I thought; however, the question is *"where* do they get the justification for doing so?" That was the response I had in mind.

There is a big difference between a man deviating from his religion to commit an injustice, and one who has a book telling him to do so. And that's what I wanted to explain at the time. I wanted explain the differences between the Quran and the Bible in relation to racism and oppression. I wanted to show that there was no way possible to compare the Islamic world with the Judeo-Christian world when it came to slavery and oppression (especially of African peoples). I wanted to let Mathew know that the people that enslaved and oppressed his ancestors for centuries were not facing Mecca to pray and reading the Quran. Unfortunately, it was a burning argument, and any word out of my mouth was just gasoline.

Since Mathew never read the Quran and knew little about Islamic history, I wanted to give him some literature that was simple, yet direct to the point. Although I had read hundreds of books, I never read one that intricately explained the positions of Islam and the Judeo-Christian religions

Universal Brotherhood: Quranic solutions to overcome racism and oppression

on this subject; therefore, I decided to write a book of my own—for the "Mathews" of the world.

Some say that the Quran encourages the Muslims to fight the idolaters; however, fighting them was only prescribed out of defense after the Muslims were forced out of their homes in Mecca. Secondly, there are millions of Muslims living in the West who are amongst the most law-abiding citizens; therefore, the critics' arguments are invalid.

WHY IS A BOOK LIKE THIS NEEDED?

One Sunday, in February 2008, I took the time to interview about a dozen Muslims at a masjid in Norfolk, Virginia to get more insight on the subject. Most of the people contributed their ideas and personal experiences about the biases and discrimination that they faced. The Imam added, "We know that racism and oppression exists. Look at how they are saying that Barak Obama isn't qualified to be president because of his inexperience. But Clinton ran for two terms and the only experience he had was as a governor, not a senator like Obama, which is actually a position closer to the presidency. The issue of his race is the only dispute that people have against him. We know that racism exists. What we need is solutions to solve it."

I agreed with him—to a certain extent. I believe that we can do things that will dramatically reduce oppressive circumstances where it won't affect our everyday lives. At the same time I know that as long as there are human beings there will be racism and oppression, just like there will be theft, lying, cheating, raping, and killing.

At the end of the interview the imam went on to discuss other questions about Islam that they may have had about other issues. However, every time he called on someone they came right back to the subject of race and oppression. It was like they were addicted to the idea and kept chasing it like it was a high: something that they had longed to talk about, but no one had the courage to bring it to the table.

So, I decided to stick with the project to satisfy this demand and:

1) To end the confusion that many people have about the source of the racial or social injustices that they are victims of here in America,

through analyzing Biblical scriptures that were influential in shaping the philosophical outlook of the Judeo-Christian West.
2) To offer sound and effective Quranic solutions to change these oppressive circumstances and their effects.
3) To explain how the Islamic concept of family unity prevents man from falling into oppressive circumstances.
4) To break down institutional racism by displaying traps so smooth that they snare the wisest of people.
5) To explain the roots and differences between Black Nationalism and Islam (as was introduced by the Prophet Muhammad (ص)).
6) Briefly address usury and how Islamic banking and business procedures are answers for all people in the West to reverse their economic conditions.
7) To address these issues in detail and illustrate various strategies so that people can either take the steps that I offer or understand their situation and devise strategies that fit their own personal needs.

WHAT SHOULD THE READER EXPECT?

I begin by examining both the Bible and the Quran's message towards racism and oppression, considering that these are the foundations of Islamic and Judeo-Christian religions. By showing their different natures it is easier to understand the societies that were built on these texts because they serve as blue prints.

Secondly, I examine the role that these texts played into the orchestration of slavery and oppression throughout history. Because slavery, discrimination, and oppression appear to be institutions of the past, I show how theological racism and oppression are still applied, affecting everyone: men, women, whites, blacks, etc.

The reader should keep in mind that although African American experiences are used, this is not a book for black people or an anti-white book. Many whites will appreciate this work. Especially the ones that have taken student, home, and car loans and done all the other things that society preaches are the keys to success, but find themselves scuffling on the treadmill of life just to survive. Some people will probably disagree no matter how much sound evidence is presented because they will either wrongly interpret this as a personal attack against them or their religion, or simply because they feel that they are on the beneficiary and not victim side of the race argument. And of course, the man with the knife poked into his flesh does the screaming, not the poker.

I believe that the following will also appreciate this work:

1) Educated minorities that run into glass ceilings after acquiring all the credentials to climb the ladder of success.
2) People looking for closure between the races.
3) History buffs.
4) People who are racially profiled and searched for drugs and humiliated during routine traffic stops.
5) Women open to pursue a role other than what is customary in the West.
6) Intelligent people of color who are often marginalized due to their high level of intellect, who face the dilemma of breaking cultural norms.
7) Disenfranchised felons who want to understand how they got into their dilemma, and want solutions on how to get out of it.
8) Skeptics that want to test the authority of this book and the Quran's ability to make real social change.

However, critics may say that President Obama having an African father is proof that racism is just a thing of the past; meaning, a man of African descent can make it to the most powerful position in the nation. But the question is "out of the millions of African American Christians who were born and raised in the United States who could have become president, why did it take Barak *Hussein* Obama, a man with a Muslim father, who spent part of his childhood in the most populous Muslim nation in the world (Indonesia), to succeed in becoming the president of the United States?"

There are a lot of different opinions. However, the fact is that he won at the ballot box. In his speech during the Democratic Con-vention in 2004 he said:

> Now even as we speak, there are those who are preparing to divide us -- the spin masters, the negative ad peddlers who embrace the politics of "anything goes." Well, I say to them tonight, there is not a liberal America and a conservative America -- there is the United States of America. There is not a Black America and a White America and Latino America and Asian America -- there's the United States of America.

His words had a dramatic impact on the masses. But why was this speech a magnet to many voters? For one, it was totally different from African American Christian leaders of the past who focused on ethnic divisions and catering to the needs of the *black community*. The whole concept of looking at humanity as one is Islamic. There are over fifty Islamic nations in the world, and not one of them require their citizens to choose what ethnic group they belong to how the United States does on job applications, driver's licenses, and other documents.

I am sure that when President Obama grew up in Indonesia he was able to play with children different from him without him being attacked with racial slurs and hatred as many African Americans experienced back during the sixties when he was young. He even said that those were the most memorable years of his life. He took this experience with him and was able to look at all people within the same light: as equals.

Therefore, the bulk of this work deals with this equality that the *Quran* prescribes. Whether the reader is a skeptic to Islam being an egalitarian religion, or a Muslim who wants to have a deeper understanding of the concept of universal brotherhood, everyone should keep in mind the title of the book while reading it: Universal Brotherhood: a *Quranic* approach to overcoming racism and oppression. I don't say a Muslim approach, because what Muslims do and what the Quran teaches are two entirely different things. I don't in anyway want to portray that Muslims are a sacred people, or that *Muslims* should be followed. This book is about the *text* of the Quran and its potential to be a cure for social inequality. However, there are times when I do refer to Muslim or Christian societies merely to show the influence of the Bible or Quran on the actions of the followers. The work ends with simple Quranic solutions that can be applied by *anyone* to reverse the effects of bigotry and oppression, whether they are Muslims or not. I do this from the victim's stand point to let him or her know that they have the potential as an individual to make change in society.

In some cases I refer to certain things in their original Arabic name because they cannot be translated accurately and retain the same meaning in English. Likewise, I use certain words interchangeable such as *Black* and *African American*; *White* or *European*; *God* or *Allah*. The word *African* is also not applied to only those who have black or dark brown skin, but to anyone indigenous to the continent of Africa: Egyptians, Berbers, Arabs, etc. I also use Arabic abbreviations in parenthesis after mentioning the name of God, prophets, imams, and other important peoples:

(ع) 'alaihi salaam.	Peace be upon him.
(ص) Sallalahu 'alaihi wa alihi wa salaam.	Blessings and peace upon him and his progeny.
(س) Subhana wa ta'ala	Glorified and exalted
(ر) Radi Allahu 'anhu.	May Allah be pleased with him.

The only request that I have is that the reader approach this work patiently as a free thinker. Humility and patience lead to learning. Anyone who thinks that they know everything there is to know about the Quran, Muslims, racism, and oppression should still take the time to read this book because many of the ideas and solutions prescribed are unique and not professed by any Muslims in the manner that I do. At times I come with my own personal experiences and solutions that I use which makes this a unique work. This book should be read from cover to cover to understand it correctly, letting go of all prejudices and superstitions before the first page is read. It's like watching a movie: you have to patiently sit through the slow parts because you know that it will be worth it at the end when everything comes together and makes sense. I spent a lot of time in the editing process to make sure that it was an easy and interesting read. Despite what side of the argument readers have been on, most agreed that it was enjoyable.

CHAPTER 1

The Bible and the Quran: Pillars of the world

THE QURAN AND ITS MESSAGE

The Quran teaches that Islam was sent to mankind the same way that Judaism and Christianity were sent to the Christians and Jews: through a messenger appointed by God. Islam's messenger was Muhammad Ibn Abdullah (ص), born in the city of Mecca 570 A.D. Just as the Jews and Christians have their holy books that are written by those inspired by God, the Muslims also have a holy book, the Quran, revealed to the Prophet of Islam by God, Allah (س), through the angel Gabriel (Jibreel). According to Islamic teachings, Allah (س) sent the Quran to the Prophet Muhammad (ص) just as he sent the Torah to Moses (ع), Psalms to David (ع), and Gospel to Jesus (ع). The Prophet Muhammad (ص) was to be the seal of the prophets, with none to follow him with the task of bringing forth new revelation from Allah (س). The message of the Quran and the Prophet Muhammad (ص) was based on the complete submission to one god, and to bring forth the correct teachings of the rightly appointed messengers who preceded him.

Islam teaches that the previous books were tampered with by the heirs of the Judeo-Christian religions, who were entrusted with the task of safeguarding and protecting the original message of Allah (س). Therefore,

Islam teaches that the Quran was sent to clarify and explain what was true and false in the Bible, by emphasizing those truths that remained in it; and by clarifying, or omitting those things considered clear deviations of the original Biblical texts.

The Quran was revealed to bring justice to all of mankind. Although it brought forth new revelation in the name of Islam, it was not revealed to slander the scriptures that preceded it. The Quran was revealed as a *Furqan*, which means a *differentiator between right and wrong*. Its purpose was to explain and confirm what came before it, as mentioned in the Quran:

> And this Quran is not such as to be forged by (anyone) besides God, but is a confirmation of (the scriptures) that went before it and (the clearest) explanation of the Book, there is no doubt in it, (it is) from the Lord of the worlds. (10:37).

Amongst the Quran's confirmations and explanations of scriptures that came before it are those in relation to the justness of Allah (س) towards his creations. According to the Quran, Allah (س) judges every individual for his or her own individual actions, punishing or rewarding them separately for whatever deeds they have performed. Therefore, anyone can live a noble or dishonorable life if he or she so chooses, despite ones race, socio-economic background, or geographical location.

However; the Bible gravitates towards the view that certain groups such as the Hebrews (Israelites) have a preferential status in the eyes of God based on their lineage, regardless of their individual actions. This decree is made clear in the Bible, beginning with the abasement of the Prophet Abraham's oldest son Ishmael (ع) below Abraham's second son Isaac (ع).

THE CURSED AFRICAN SEED

The Bible reads that Abraham (ع) was born in the ancient city of Ur (located in present-day Iraq). He then migrated to the land of Canaan, which was the land west of the Jordan River, now known as Israel. He wanted his descendants and himself to rule over their own land. There were two problems: he had no descendants, and no land for them to inherit. Canaan was already occupied by the Canaanites, and his elderly wife, Sarah, was unable to bear children. So, the Bible reads that during a dream these two problems were solved.

During his time it was a custom for two leaders to make an agreement with one another by performing a special ritual. This ritual would consist of the slaughtering of several animals, where their bodies would be divided into two. Then, a path would be made, where one half of an animal's body would be on the left side of the path, and the other half of its body would be laid on the right. Each animal's half would be laid next another animal's half. Then, the leaders would walk down this path, between the halves, similarly to how a bride and groom would walk down the aisle with the congregation of people on opposing sides. The ceremony represented that the fate of the two people going down the path would be that of the dead carcasses if they should deviate from their vow.

During a vision in Abraham's dream, he was to have been promised by God, that one day his descendants would inherit the land of Canaan, which was inhabited by the Canaanites at that time (Gen. Ch.15). Like most important pacts of that time, this covenant was sealed by Abraham walking between this path of dead carcasses, followed by God also going down this path in the image of a burning kettle:

1. After these things the word of the LORD came unto Abram in a vision, saying, Fear not, Abram: I am thy shield, and thy exceeding great reward.
2. And Abram said, LORD God, what wilt thou give me, seeing I go childless, and the steward of my house is this Eliezer of Damascus?
3. And Abram said, Behold, to me thou hast given no seed: and, lo, one born in my house is mine heir.
4. And, behold, the word of the LORD came unto him, saying, This shall not be thine heir; but he that shall come forth out of thine own bowels shall be thine heir.
5. And he brought him forth abroad, and said, Look now toward heaven, and tell the stars, if thou be able to number them: and he said unto him, So shall thy seed be.
6. And he believed in the LORD; and he counted it to him for righteousness.

7. And he said unto him, I am the LORD that brought thee out of UR of the Chaldees, to give thee this land to inherit it.
8. And he said, LORD God, whereby shall I know that I shall inherit it?
9. And he said unto him, Take me a heifer of three years old, and a she goat of three years old, and a ram of three years old, and a turtledove, and a young pigeon.
10. And he took unto him all these, and divided them in the midst, and laid each piece one against another: but the birds divided he not.
11. And when the fowls came down upon the carcasses, Abram drove them away.
12. And when the sun was going down, a deep sleep fell upon Abram; and, lo, a horror of great darkness fell upon him.
13. And he said unto Abram, know of a surety that thy seed shall be a stranger in a land that is not theirs, and shall serve them; and they shall afflict them four hundred years;
14. And also that nation, whom they shall serve, will I judge: and afterward shall they come out with great substance.
15. And thou shalt go to thy fathers in peace; thus shalt be buried in a good old age.
16. But in the fourth generation they shall come hither again: for the iniquity of the Amorites is not yet full.
17. And it came to pass, that, when the sun went down, and it was dark, behold a smoking furnace, and a burning lamp that passed between those pieces.
18. In the same day the LORD made a covenant with Abram, saying, Unto thy seed have I given this land, from the river of Egypt unto the great river, the river Euphrates: (Genesis 15:1-18)

In order for him to fulfill this Covenant, Sarah advised him to marry and seek intimacy with his younger African slave, Hagar. After the marriage, Hagar gave birth to Abraham's son, Ishmael. During that era, the right of inheritance and succession to authority was give to the first born son; however, Sarah (the Hebrew wife) became jealous of Hagar and then asked God to bless her with a son in the same way that Hagar was blessed with one. God granted her that wish; she conceived a son: Isaac. Despite the fact that Ishmael was the first born and was conceived so that Abraham could fulfill Covenant with God, his birth-right of inheritance was revoked once Isaac was born, leaving Isaac as the one to inherit that which was promised to Abraham (according to the Quran, Ishmael is the chosen son).

The only difference between Isaac and Ishmael was that Isaac was the son of a Hebrew, while Ishmael was the son of an African (Egyptian). Because of this difference in lineage, Isaac is spoken of very highly; whereas, Ishmael is predestined to spend his life in a state of ignorance and strife, as described in the Biblical dialogue between Hagar and the angel who was sent by God (Gen. Ch. 16:1):

11. And the Angel also said, "You are now pregnant and will give birth to a son. You are to name him Ishmael. For the Lord has heard about your misery...
22. "This son of your will be a wild one—free and untamed as a wild donkey! He will be against him. Yes, he will live at odds with the rest of his brothers."[1]

Notice how the same term, donkey, is used in the Quran, however, towards those who possess knowledge, but refuse to apply it:

The similitude of those who were placed under the Torah, and they held (followed) it not, is as the similitude of a donkey bearing books (on its back); wretched is the similitude of the people who belie the signs of God; and God guides not the unjust people. (Quran 62:5)

Unlike the Bible, here we see that the emphasis is placed on the action of the individual, and not on his or her lineage. Although both books use the word *donkey* to describe an ignorant person, the Quran explains that this ignorance is due to that person's reluctance to adhere to and apply the knowledge that he or she possesses. The Quran teaches that the person who has obtained knowledge, but refrains from applying it will, indeed, spend life in the midst of hardships and in opposition to his environment as mentioned. The Quran teaches that qualities such as ignorance and immorality can't be inherited through bloodlines, but are results of one's individual decisions. In Islam, the only way that one can inherit such qualities is through imitating the ways of that individual's forefathers who may have been in error:

> 3. Verily thou (O' Muhammad art of the apostles, sent by God)
> 4. On the straight path
> 5. Sent by the All-Mighty the All-Merciful,
> 6. So that thou may warn a people whose fathers were not warned, and who therefore are headless (of the truth). (Quran 36:3-6)

Islam teaches that no matter how ignorant or corrupt a person's ways may be, they can be broken if the individual truly wishes to change. The Quran explains that anyone, despite their ethnicity, can pursue the path of enlightenment and prosper through that knowledge obtained if he or she so chooses. However, man has been placed in degrees where some people have IQs that are higher than others. Some people are even born with mental or physical impairments that prohibit them from achieving what the average person can, but these are scenarios that all races are subjected to. According to the Quran, it is our actions that determine our rewards; although our natural abilities do play a significant role as well. Even the Prophet Muhammad (ص) himself was a man chosen to bring the last Revelation of God because of his merits, not because of his Arab ancestry:

> 21. Indeed there is for you in the apostle of God (Muhammad) an excellent pattern (of conduct) for him who hopeth in and the latter day and remembered much. (Quran 33:21)
> 159. Thus it is a mercy of God that thou art lenient to them; had thou been severe and hard-hearted, they would surely have dispersed away from around Thee… Quran 33:159)

Therefore, the Biblical abasement of Ishmael below his brother Isaac, on account of his African ancestry, is considered unacceptable in the religion of Islam.

Besides the Biblical account of Ishmael's inferior position, the Quran goes on to address yet another biased account in the Biblical text. This second account is where Noah (ع) curses his son Ham and condemns Ham's descendants to be the slaves for the descendants of Noah's other two sons, Japheth and Shem. (Gen. 9:25-27)[1]

After the great flood the earth was to be repopulated by Noah's three sons: Japheth, Shem, and Ham. The Bible describes how Noah once fell asleep in the nude while he was in a state of drunkenness. Ham saw him naked (some people argue that the text hints he may have done more than just watch). Ham then went back to his brothers and informed them of what happened. When Noah awoke, his two sons Japheth and Shem then informed their father, Noah, of what Ham did. Noah cursed Ham and condemned his descendants to be the servants for the descendants of Japheth and Shem: "And he said, Cursed be Canaan; a servant of servants shall he be unto his brethren" (Gen. 9:25-27).

The descendants of Japheth were to become the Caucasian and Indo-European races. The descendants of Shem were to be the Arameans, Hebrews, Persians, Assyrians, and Arabians: the Semitic peoples. Ham was the father of four sons: Cush, Mizraim, Canaan, Phut. They were described as the progenitors of the southern peoples of the planet (Africans). Cush was the forefather of the Ethiopians; Canaan of the Canaanites (the pre-Israelite inhabitants of Palestine); Mizraim of the Egyptians; and Phut of a Libyan people (Gen. 10:1, 6-20). Egypt (Africa) is mentioned several times in the Psalms as the "land of Ham" (Psalms 105:23, 27; 106:22).

Ham is defined in the *Practical Bible Dictionary and Concordance* by James P. Boyd as being the father of Cush. Cush is identified as being *black*. Therefore, the descendants of Ham, which include Cush and his descendants, are defined as *the black African races, and the servants for the Indo-European and Semitic races.*[2]

Some may argue that the curse applied only to Canaan; however, the Bible says that: "Know therefore that the Lord the God, he is God, the

---

[1] It is a theory that the story of Ham was invented from the Israelites' need for a scriptural premise for their conquest over the Canaanites that already lived in the land. There is also some debate whether this curse was placed only on Canaan or on all of his (Ham's) descendants. No matter who it is placed on, or for what reason, we see the nature of the Bible bends towards people being sentenced to servitude because of their lineage. This is not in contrast with the rest of the Bible which places much emphasis on tribal purity and genealogies.

faithful God, which keepeth Covenant and mercy with them that love him and keep his commandments to a thousand generations... (Deut. 7:9)." This means that this curse is still applicable today to those living in Watts, Bedford Stuyvesant, or South Chicago. Writer Claude Brown captured the personification of blacks in Harlem living under Judeo-Christian oppression in his book *Descendants of Ham*.

This Biblical incident of Ham's descendants being the servants for other peoples was, and still is used to justify black slavery. Brigham Young, the second president of The Church of Jesus Christ of Latter-day Saints, was amongst the strongest advocates of this curse. When asked by journalist and political leader Horace Greeley about what the church's stance on slavery was, he answered, "We consider it of divine institution and not to be abolished until the curse pronounced on Ham shall have been removed from his descendants (black African peoples)."[3]

The abolitionist Frederick Douglass, sold into slavery by his own white father, explained how the bond of blood still could not save him from the Biblical curse of Ham:

> ...Whether this prophecy is ever fulfilled or not, it is nevertheless plain that a very different-looking class of people are springing up in the south, and are now held in slavery, from those originally brought to this country from Africa; and if their increase will do no other good, it will do away the force of the argument, that God cursed Ham, and therefore American slavery is right. If the lineal descendants of Ham are alone to be scripturally enslaved, it is certain that slavery at the south must soon become unscriptural; for thousands are ushered into the world, annually, who, like myself, owe their existence to white fathers, and those fathers most frequently their own masters.[4]

The Quran denounces such beliefs of a people being cursed for the supposed sin of their ancestors, where it reads, "One shall not bear the burden of another" (17:15). The chapter in the Quran that this verse was revealed is *Bani Israel, the People of Israel*—a title which indicates the group being addressed. The people of Israel felt as though God had sanctioned them above all other people in the Bible because of their lineage. Thus, this Quranic verse was revealed to clarify that no human being is to be rewarded for his or her ethnicity. One of the attributes of God in the religion of Islam is *'Adl*, which means the *Just* in Arabic. God ordaining a race below another because of their lineage is considered unjust in Islam. It is a general Islamic belief that Biblical verses reflecting racial biases are actually deviations from the original text. Such verses were clearly influenced by the Hebrews' (Israelites') desire to appoint themselves superior to other peoples. The Quran explains in detail how ethnicity and gender are irrelevant in terms of how God judges Mankind:

> O ye people! Verily We (God) have created you of a male and a female, made you in nations and tribes, that you may recognize each other; verily the most honored of you with God is the one of you who guards (himself) the most (against evil), verily God is All-Knowing, the All-Aware. (49:13)

The Quran describes how mankind is but one; all stemming from the same pair, where no one is to be favored according to sex or ethnicity. According to the Quran, people are measured according to their level of piety. The only significance of human diversity is for the purpose of recognition. Even brothers and sisters are genetically distinct from one another, despite the fact that they have the "same" blood. The Quran emphasizes that the Justness of God extends to everyone. Anyone who thinks that they are immune from his justness because they are under the umbrella of a particular race has not yet grasped the Islamic concept of *'Adl—the Justness of God*. In the Quran, all of mankind is to receive their reward according to their merit, as the Quran states: "Imposeth not God, any soul but to its (individual) ability; for it shall be (the good) what he hath acquired and against it (shall be, the evil) he hath wrought..." (Quran 2:286)

HEBREW/ISRAELITE SUPERIORITY

The actual Covenant of the Land of Canaan to the Hebrews (which occurred in one of Abraham's dreams) was a premise to justify their conquest of the Land of Canaan. Although Abraham himself never possessed the land, the Israelites—described as a "holy seed"—are given exclusive rights to this land due to their lineage (Ezra 9:2). The rights to this land was based strictly on their bloodline and not on their merit, as the Bible reads, "Understand this: therefore, it is not because of your merits that the Lord, Your God, is giving you this good land to possess, for you are a stiff-necked people" (Deut. 9:6).

The Israelites are described as being "stiff-necked" because they neglected to follow the commandments of God. In relation to character and deeds, the Israelites were no better than the people they were seizing the land from. Being descendants of Abraham—who had a *dream* that God gave him the land—gave them the right to take the land from the Canaanites and other inhabitants of that land—according to the Bible. Perhaps, one could understand their right to the land to begin with if they would have purchased it legitimately, leaving it as an inheritance for their direct descendants; however, to say that the Israelites had or have exclusive rights to the property of others because of their genealogy is considered absurd and racist to most.

This belief of the Hebrews' racial superiority is to the extent that they are instructed not to contaminate their holy seed, or bloodlines, by marrying non-Hebrews. Abraham instructed his son Isaac not to marry a Canaanite, as Isaac instructed his son Jacob not to marry a Canaanite woman as well (Gen. 24:3). Although the Hebrews could take the land of the Canaanites, marrying them was forbidden.

RIGHTEOUSNESS OVER RACE

The Quran clarifies and explains that racial superiority and segregation on the premise of ethnicity were not the true messages of the previous prophets. The Quran does not forbid racial integration. The only requirement that must be met by the one who wants to marry a Muslim is that he or she must willingly convert to Islam first:

> And marry not idolater women until they believe; a believer bondswoman is definitely better than an idolater (free) woman even though she may allure you; and give not in marriage (your women) to idolater men until they believe; a believer bondsman is better than an idolater

(free) man; even though he may allure you; they beckon (you) to (Hell) Fire, and verily God beckons (you) to the Garden and forgiveness by his leave, and makes clear His signs for men so that they may be mindful. (Quran 2:21)

According to *Tafsir Ibn Kathir* (vol.III), this verse was revealed in regards to a man named Abdullah Ibn Rawaha, who abused his African servant when he was angry. He felt guilty because of his action, so he informed the Prophet Muhammad (ص) about the incident. The Prophet (ص) replied, "Oh, Abu Abdullah! She is a believer." Abu Abdullah said, "I swear by God who has sent you with the truth, that I will free her and will marry her." After he married her there were Muslims who despised him for marrying his African servant. [5]

This was because the Muslims, who were recent converts from Polytheism, still retained many of their polytheistic biased beliefs. There were many Muslims who wanted him to marry a polytheist, on account of her supposedly noble lineage.[6]

This Quranic verse was revealed to eliminate the prejudices that the people had against one another and to place an emphasis on the importance of faith over lineage.

Islam does not consider bloodlines or family ties to be a key to the door of paradise that should not be blemished with the blood of others. Islam does, however, value family relations to the extent that it is forbidden for a Muslim to cut his or her family ties, even if they are not Muslims. The only way that it is permissible for one to cut these ties is if these non-believing family members are in clear opposition to Islam, as the Quran states, "O; ye who believe! Take ye not your fathers and brothers for friends if they love infidelity above (more than) faith; and whosoever of you make friends of them, then those it is who are the unjust (9:23)."

Here we see that the enemies of Islam are to be abandoned by the Muslims no matter who they may be. In the beginning of the Prophet Muhammad's (ص) mission, his uncle, Abu Lahab, used to curse him because of his opposition to Islam. Eventually, a whole chapter in the Quran was revealed condemning both Abu Lahab and his wife, despite the fact that they were both Arabs and relatives of the Prophet (ص) himself.

Meanwhile, the Bible gives numerous examples of God's unconditional forgiveness for the Israelite's (Hebrews) transgressions. God forgives them in the Bible and continues to favor them over all other peoples.

Islam extends to all people. Although the Prophet Muhammad was an Arab, the Quran does not refrain from warning those Arabs, who neglected their Islamic obligations, from the punishment to come:

> And come with excuses from the dwellers of the desert (Arabs) that permission may be given to them, and say (at home) those who lied to God and his Apostle; unto those of them who disbelieved shall shortly reach a grievous chastisement. (Quran 9:90)

This is in conflict with the Bible, where God favors the Israelites unconditionally over all other peoples. Even Jesus (ع) was described in the Bible as being exclusively sent for "the lost sheep of the house of Israel (Israelites)":

> 22. And behold, a woman of Canaan came out of the same coasts, and cried unto him, saying, Have mercy on me, O Lord, thou Son of David; my daughter is grievously vexed with a devil.
> 23. But he answered and said, I am not sent but unto the lost sheep of the house of Israel...
> 25. Then came she and worshipped him, saying, Lord, help me.
> 26. But he answered and said, It is not meet to take the children's bread, and cast it to dogs. (Math. 15:16-26)

According to the Bible, Jesus was only sent to assist the Israelites. This verse refers to the Israelites as *children*, Jesus' blessings are *bread*, and the Canaanites are called *dogs*. In other words, Jesus giving the Canaanites blessings would be equivalent to taking bread from children and giving it to dogs.

The Quran, on the other hand, explains how the Prophet Muhammad (ص) was sent for all of mankind, and not only for the Arab people: "Whatever good befalls thee (O' man!) it is from God and whatever evil befalls thee, it is from thyself; we have sent thee (O' Our Apostle Muhammad!) unto mankind as (our Apostle) and God is sufficient a witness (thereof) (Quran 4:79)."

THE RIGHTS OF THE OPPRESSED

The Quran explains that the messengers of God were sent to administer equality to society, not to bestow privileges upon one group while depriving others of those same benefits.

For instance, if we look at the word justice, we see that it is often associated with scales, as in the term "the scales of justice." In Arabic the word for *justice* is *mizan* which also means a *scale*: an instrument used to measure or balance. In Islam justice is administered through measuring mankind with equality and balance. It does not permit a disproportionate distribution of land, property, wealth, or rights according to ethnicity.

If land property, wealth, or rights were to be taken from an individual or a group, the Quran permits those who were wronged to reclaim that which has been taken or to seek the equivalent through being compensated by those who have transgressed. At the same time, the Quran permits the victim to use reasoning to choose between either retaliation or forgiveness for the transgression:

> 40. And the recompense for an evil shall be an ill-return like unto it, but (if) one pardoneth and amends, his reward is incumbent on God; Verily he loves not the unjust.
> 41. And whoseoever defendeth himself (in avenging) after being oppressed, then against these there is no way (to blame).
> 42. The way (to blame) is against those who do injustice unto the people and transgress in the earth unjustly; these, for them shall be a painful chastisement.
> 43. and indeed whosoever remains patient and forgives, verily this is an act of great resolution. (40:40-43) 43.

However, the Bible prohibits the victim of an offense from defending him or herself and from seeking compensation for that which has been wrongfully taken:

> 27. But I say unto you which hear. Love your enemies, do good to them which hate you.

28. Bless them that curse you, and pray for them which despitefully use you.
29. And unto him that smiteth thee on the one cheek offer also the other; and him that taketh away the cloak forbid not to take they coat also... (Luke 6:27)

This disproportionate favoring of property and rights favors those who possess authority in the Bible. The Bible encourages the Christians to accept persecution, and to confront injustice by being generous to the persecutor instead of seeking compensation for the injustice that had occurred, as the Bible reads, "But I say unto you, love your enemies, bless them that curse you, do good to them that hate you, and pray for them which despitefully use you and persecute you (Mathew 5:44)."

The Quran liberates and frees the Muslim from the yoke of oppression by placing no blame on the person wronged if he or she seeks to avenge an injustice that has occurred against them. The Quran does not prohibit people from defending themselves or preventing themselves from being oppressed:

39. And (those) who when afflicteth them any great wrong, they get helped by themselves.
40. And the recompense for and evil shall be an ill-reward is incumbent on God; verily he loveth not the unjust.
41. And whosoever defendeth himself (in avenging) after being oppressed, then against these there is no way to blame. (Quran 40:39)

The Quran does not condone exploitation and oppression. The Quran even opposes those in authority if they are oppressing or exploiting others. True Islam professes that it is the obligation of those that are exploited and oppressed to seize the power from those who abuse it. In Islam, it is incumbent that the believer obeys the commandments of the Quran. If tyrannical rulers are in opposition to the laws of the Quran, the Muslims are allowed to free themselves from their rule. Contrary to the Bible, the Quran does not equate the laws of those in authority with the laws of God in terms of absolute submission. The following verse illustrates how the Bible has commanded the Christians to obey those in authority with the same reverence that they would obey God himself:

1. Let every soul be subject unto the higher powers. For there is no power but God.
2. Whosoever therefore resisteth the power, resisteth the ordinance of God: and they that resisteth shall receive to themselves damnation. (Romans 13:1-1)

Of course, following laws is essential to the cohesiveness of all societies; man must remember that segregation, the prohibition of mixed marriages and other Jim Crow laws, not to even mention the Holocaust, were inhumane results of unquestionable adherence to the law. Absolute submission to the law is forbidden in Islam when it transgresses against the rights of other people. The Quran instructs mankind to enjoin what is good and forbid what is wrong in all circumstances (3:109). Therefore, those who support corrupt authorities or fail to oppose them are equivalent to their oppressors because their support or passiveness actually fuels the tyrant's campaign of injustice, leaving them with no right to voice their grievances—which are self-inflicted through submissiveness.

CONCLUSION

The Quran's purpose was to explain and confirm that which came before it: that man was given the right to pursue the path that leads to social equality. It also explains that humanity is to be judged by God according to piety, not race. It was sent to free people from the fabricated Biblical verses that rearranged the system of equality and fairness previously revealed by God. Islam teaches that some have manipulated the Bible so that it could serve their particular purposes. These Biblical verses were to subdue the masses and exalt one group above the rest—according to race. This is not to say that all Jews and Christians are racists and oppressors, but that the Bible has specific verses that open up that avenue for those who wish to be.

Even if opponents could successfully refute the claim that the Bible has sanctioned servitude for African Peoples it still leaves the fact that a mere dream gives an entire race of people the right to take land from another people. Secondly, curses are sent down through many generations to innocent people while blessings are inherited by those who are no different than the supposedly cursed.

Although discrimination and oppression are wrong and illogical for most people to accept, they thrive on the premise that it is what has been ordained by God. The Quran was sent to undo the damage done by those who tampered with the original scriptures. The Quran acts as the true abolitionist by freeing people from the bondage of false doctrines that permit and advocate injustices to exist and thrive within the hearts of mankind and their institutions.

The Quran can be a superior weapon to combat these social injustices that are deep-rooted in today's world. It can act as a clarifier and redeemer for those who look towards divine scripture for guidance to improve our social conditions that are a result of what today's most dominant societies have been built on—the Bible—which will be explained in the following chapters.

CHAPTER 2

Racist Blueprint

It would be useless to refer to Biblical texts without showing how they influence the injustices that we see today. There are thousands of examples that I could use to defend this claim. However, America has combined many different Judeo-Christian cultures, experiences, and beliefs, forming a nation with a general atmosphere, attitude, and culture that best reflects a genuine Judeo-Christian society.

It was America's founding fathers who laid down the initial blueprint for the society to come. They were people whose ways of thinking and mandates were heavily influenced by the Bible as described by the historian Clarence B. Carson:

> The bent to have a written constitution ran strongly in the American blood. So strong was their commitment that they would also soon have a government without a constitution as a man appear in public without his clothes. This bent, or tradition can be traced to many sources. Americans were above all, a people of the book—the written word—, the bible. There was the Puritan idea, too, of the Covenant, an agreement between man and man and between man and God... [1]

This American idea of having a Covenant between man and man, and man and God, was of the same nature as the Covenant between the descendants of Abraham and God in the Bible. The same way the descendants of Abraham believed that they were God's holy seed (Ezra 9:2) and sanctioned by God to seize the land of Canaan, is the same way that the founding fathers of America felt that they were a divine people, and that America was sanctioned to them by God; sanctioned to them down to the thousandth generation as mentioned in Thomas Jefferson's first Inaugural Address:

> ....Let us, then, with courage and confidence pursue our own federal and republican principles, our attachment to union and representative government. Kindly separated by nature and a wide ocean from the extermination havoc of one quarter of the globe: too high minded to endure the degradations of the others; possessing a chosen country, with room enough for our descendants to the thousandth and thousandth generation...[2]

The language used by Jefferson reflects his Biblical convictions in regards to 'God sanctioning land to a specific race. This idea was undoubtedly influenced by the following Biblical verse, where God confirms his Covenant to the Israelites—down to a thousand generations: "Know therefore that the Lord the God, he is God, the faithful God, which keepeth Covenant and mercy with them that love him and keep his commandments to a thousand generations...(Deut. 7:9)."

This theory that God had ordained some races above others extended far beyond the hearts of the American people. It became a documented covenant, just like the Bible. This contemporary documented covenant is known as the Constitution of the United States of America. Like the Bible, this Constitution, or Covenant, has even refused to recognize the intrinsic value of non-whites until they only had three-fifths the representation of whites (Article I, Section 2). The three-fifths law of the Constitution abased people of African descent below the rest of society in the same way that the descendants of Ham (Africans) were made subservient and abased below the rest of society during Biblical times. This is often referred to as the Three-fifths Compromise where delegates against slavery wanted to only count the free people of each state.

Even Abraham Lincoln—who is portrayed to be one of the greatest rivals of slavery and liberators for African Americans—still expressed his belief that the white European race had been ordained superior over the African race; the same way that God ordained a superior position to the descendants of Shem and Japheth over the descendants of Ham (the African peoples). The following is a piece from one of his speeches that reflects his sentiments:

> ....I am not nor ever have been in favor of making voters or jurors of negroes, nor qualifying them to hold office, nor to intermarry with white people; and I will say in addition to this that there is a physical difference between the white and black races which I believe will forever forbid the two races living together on terms of social and political equality. And inasmuch as they cannot so live, while they do remain together there must be the position of superior and inferior and I as much as any other man am in favor of having the superior position assigned to the white race...[3]

Like so many other Christian forefathers of America, Abraham Lincoln (whose picture remains on U.S. currency) also believed in the divine sanction of power given to whites over blacks. This was clearly an oppressively racist belief, which he expressed most comfortably amongst the American Christian public, despite how just history has conjured him to be. The fact that he is recognized by many as being one of the greatest liberators for African Americans, but at the same time believing that the superior position is assigned to the white race, only validates the claim that racism and the desire to oppress is often in the hearts of the most liberal minded of Christians.

Not only were such ideas possessed by the leaders and founders of America, but they were commonly expressed by the body of the American people and not restricted to Blacks. Anyone with pigment was labeled as being one who could do evil, but yet show no shame, on the premise that the Bible reads, "Were they ashamed when they had committed abomination? Nay, they were not at all ashamed, neither could they blush: therefore they shall fall among them that fall: at the same time thath I visit them they shall be cast down, saith the Lord (Jeremiah 6:15)."

Notice how the American philosopher Josiah Royce (1885-1916) describes the injustices meted out to the *Californios* (*Native Hispanic Californians*), by the Christian American settlers:

> We did not massacre them wholesale, as Turks might have massacred them: that treatment we reserved for the digger Indians... Nay, the foreign miners, being civilized men, generally received "fair trials"... Whenever they were accused. It was, however, considered safe by an average lynching jury in those days to convict a "greaser:"on very moderate evidence if none better could be had... It served him right, of course. He had no business, as an alien, to come to the land that God had given us. And if he was a Native Californian, or "greaser", the so much the worse for him. He was so much the more our born foe; we hated this whole degenerate, thieving landowning lazy and discontented race.[4]

The idea of racial superiority being the premise and the right to take land from other people was undoubtedly influenced by the Bible, or as Josiah Royce expressed it, "the land that God had given us."

Here, we see how the American people used the judicial system as a tool to systematically orchestrate a racist form of oppression against the *Californio* and digger Indians, who were the rightful owners of the land. This was almost identical to how the Israelites used the Bible as a tool to seize the land from the Canaanites, who were also the rightful owners of the land of Canaan.

Not only was racism and oppression advocated by the forefathers and early settlers of America, but it was also propagated by the church as well. The church often advocated the exploitation of blacks through slavery. Slave traders who were well versed in the Bible used to often quote scriptures to justify the black slave trade on the premise that blacks were the descendants of Ham and that slavery was ordained for them by God.

In fact, the church played such a great role in advocating racism and the oppression of African peoples until the church became the main target for abolitionist movements as described in Frederick Douglas' speech *What to the Slave is the Fourth of July?*:

....But the church of this country is not only indifferent to the wrongs of the slave, it actually takes sides with the oppressors. It has made itself the bulwark of American slavery, and the shield of American slave hunters. Many of its most eloquent Divines, who stand as the very lights of the church, have shamelessly given the sanction of religion and the Bible to the whole slave system. They have taught that man may, properly, be a slave; that the relation of master and slave is ordained of God; that send back and escaped bondman to his master is clearly the duty of all of the followers of the Lord Jesus Christ...[5]

Although Frederick Douglas himself was a Christian, he could not deny the fact that the church was a strong supporter of racism and oppression. There were, however, Christian ministers who have made great strides to abolish slavery, as described by Mason T. Lowance in his book *Against Slavery: An Abolitionist Reader*:

Their campaign was often propelled by their own personal view on the moral wrongs of slavery rather that any passages from the Bible that condemned slavery...abolitionists and antislavery advocates both used the Bible as an antislavery resource, they were less able to turn to Scripture for precedent and example than the proslavery writers because the Old Testament, and some parts of the New Testament offered historical precedents for the divine sanction of slavery.[6]

Mason T. Lowance proceeds to explain how the antislavery advocates had to actually base their arguments on their own personal beliefs rather than any Biblical text, because no such antislavery scriptures existed:

Antislavery advocates likewise followed the sermon format of text, doctrine, and application. However, their emphasis was less on the exegesis of text and more on the moral application of the spiritual principles inherent on the text to the social and political issue of slavery in America. For example, in James Freeman Clarke's Thanksgiving Day sermon of 1842, a special-occasion sermon that would have been attended by many more listeners than the usual Sunday sermon, we find very little exegesis but long passages emphasizing the moral wrongs of slavery...[7]

The Bible was such a powerful tool to advocate racism and oppression, until it was not only used by preachers to justify black slavery, but it was also used to show the victims of those injustices that their situation was divinely sanctioned by God. Thus, it was the obligation of the victims to appreciate these injustices done to them. Therefore, seeking compensation for these injustices would be clear violations of the word of God. Christianization was one of the first steps used by those in power to keep those who were oppressed compliant to the demands of the oppressors.

In such places as Massachusetts, proto-Indian reservations were established by the early European settlers for the purpose of segregation and reeducation, as described by Roger Daniel in *Coming to America: a history of immigration and ethnicity in America*: "These plantations were referred to by the colonists as 'Indian plantations,' 'Indian villages,' or 'praying towns,' as the last designation suggests, Christianization was often part of the 'taming' process."[8]

We can also see this religious methodology of "taming" in the teachings of the most prominent of the early colonial thinkers—Cotton Mather's in particular.

Cotton Mather was born in Boston, Massachusetts (1663-1728). He was a minister who wrote and published more than 400 remarkable works. He was the most renowned and honored of all of the New England Puritans. He enrolled in Harvard at the age of 12, passing entrance exams that required the reading and writing of Latin, and the declining of Greek nouns and verbs. He received and M.A. degree by the age of 18; formally ordained as a minister at 22. His father was Increase Mather, who was a minister and president of Harvard College. His identity and life's achievements can be found in Robert Middle Dauff's *The Mathers: three Generations of Puritan Intellectuals*, (1971): Kenneth Silverman's *The Life and Times of Cotton Mather*, which Silverman won a Pulitzer Prize for in 1984.

Through his advanced works, Cotton Mather was very influential in shaping the attitudes and culture of Americans. He was amongst the minute few that placed an emphasis on development through rewarding good behavior, instead of punishment for bad behavior. In relation to slavery, he acknowledged the value of the Negro, and advocated instilling in them obedience through Christianization. The following is an example of the slave-making instructions he delivered to slave owners:

> Yea the pious Masters, that have instituted their Servants in Christian Piety, will even in this Life have a sensible Recompense. The more Serviceable and Obedient and obliging Behaviour [of] their Servants unto them, will be a sensible & a notable Recompense. Be assured, Sirs; your Servants will be the Better Servants, for being made Christian Servants. To Christianize them aright, will be to fill them with all Goodness. Christianity is nothing but a very Mass of Universal Goodness. Were your servants well tinged with the spirit of Christianity, it would render them exceedingly Dutiful unto their masters, exceeding Patient under their Masters, exceeding faithful in their Business, and Afraid of Speaking or doing anything that may justly displease you...
>
> The way is now cleared for the work that is proposed: that excellent WORK, THE INSTRUCTION OF THE NEGROES IN THE CHRISTIAN RELIGION...[9]

A good example of how Christianization subdued people into accepting slavery as a mercy of God was in the case of Phillis Wheatley (1753-1784), who was brought from Africa to America as a slave during her childhood. Unlike most slaves, she was more than fortunate to have masters that provided her with an education that allowed her to become internationally renowned for her poetry and antislavery sentiments. Despite the fact that American slavery was such an appalling injustice, Phillis Wheatley, surprisingly enough, referred to it as being a mercy from God because it introduced her to Christianity. She was then paraded around Europe as clear proof to the world that slavery was actually a mercy from God for the African peoples. The following is one of her many famous poems called *On Being Brought from Africa to America*:

> Twas mercy brought me from my pagan land,
> Taught my benighted soul to understand
> That there's a God, that there's a savior too
> Once, I redemption neither sought nor knew.

Some view our sable race with scornful eye.
"Their color is a diabolic dye."
Remember, Christians, Negroes, black as Cain,
May be refined, and join the angelic train.[10]

CONTEMPORARY OPPRESSION

Christianization was not only a tool used to influence people during slavery to accept the injustices meted out to them; it was also used to keep the masses submissive to the ruling authorities in more recent times. Even after slavery was abolished in America (1865), minorities were still persecuted and oppressed. Christian lynch mobs such as the Ku Klux Klan ran rampant throughout the whole United States, while legalized race segregation and discrimination existed until the nineteen sixties, there were many organizations that worked to stop the injustices that were taking place against minorities. Amongst those organizations was the Student Non-Violent Coordinating Committee (SNCC), who made the spotlight when they were involved in a bottle throwing incident with the police in the summer of 1966.

During the nineteen sixties, students from the Tuskegee Institute in Alabama organized and then challenged different forms of discrimination in their town of Tuskegee. In January 1966, one of the student leaders by the name of Sammy Young Jr. was murdered by a white man because he wanted to use the restroom at a gas station that was for whites only. Because of the controversial nature of the case, the trial was held in a different county where the murderer was acquitted of the crime.

Consequently, a student group held a protest in Tuskegee because of their disgust with this injustice that was orchestrated by the judicial system in Alabama. During the protest, the *non-violent* demonstrators were harassed and intimidated by the police. As a result, the protest got out of hand, and there was damage done to some property by the protestors due to the provocation of the police.

The damage done to the property was insignificant in comparison to the murder of Sammy Young Jr. and the rest of the injustices done to the African Americans of Tuskegee. However, African American Christians focused more energy on criticizing the protesters instead of the cold-blooded murderers and oppressors who created circumstances that led to such a protest. In a letter to the editor of *The Tuskegee News*, a Black woman, who was very prominent in civic affairs, describes the general submissive attitude of the majority of the African American Christian citizens of Tuskegee:

> Anyone who knows me understands that I yield to no one in dedication to equal citizenship rights. I have long worked for elimination of injustices and discrimination. I believe in the American dream—the Christian principle—of democracy for all regardless of race, color or creed. I have stood by this conviction. In recent days, especially last Saturday, the events connected with the equal rights movement did nothing for progress but only damaged the cause of responsible citizenship. I refer, of course, to the display of undisciplined and irresponsible behavior by a few young persons which was marked by rock and bottle throwing. I am ashamed by every person who set off this incident or who had any part in it... The vast majority of mature, Christian, right thinking Negro citizens regret what happened.
>
> There are many needs in the present situation. The first is responsible action and the exercise of calm judgment by every citizen. Those of us who live here and love this community have much at stake. The SNCC type from outside and the handful who are persuaded to act outside the law do not seem to understand this. We want a type of relationship, built on solid ground, which will endure through the years—a relationship depending upon mutual trust and respect. This does not derive from rowdyism and lawlessness...
>
> There was an article in last week's *Time Magazine* which referred to the recent inexcusable murder as having removed a façade which had covered up lack of progress in equal rights. Anyone who knew the voter situation here several years ago and who knows the facts today could not agree with that statement.... Sure, we have not realized all our ambitions. Certainly we have a long way to go. But the important thing is that we were on the way—that we had made remarkable progress, and that this progress had been made without violence of any type.... Tuskegee is our home, we are proud of its institutions. We insist on equality of opportunity—under law and under God—but we are not

radical street demonstrators, losing control of our good instincts. Nor will we endorse or support those who work without purpose or concern for law and order.

Let all of us—white and colored—join hands in securing justice, obedience of law and good will which will bring progress in every area of our common life.[11]

The author of this article expressed sentiments that were undoubtedly influenced by such Biblical passages as Romans 13:1, which commands people to obey the authorities as they would obey God, because they exist only through the will of God. The "turn-the-other-cheek": command is also presented (Luke 6:27). Here we also see that those of African descent are the victims of this oppression, in the same manner that the Bible curses the descendants of Ham to be subservient to the Indo-Europeans (descendants of Japheth). Moreover, it is logical to conclude that these verses directly influenced her decision to make such comments on the premise that she has labeled herself as being a devout Christian. As a Christian, the writer expresses a need for justice through obedience to the law and good will by the African American "right thinking Christians." However, it was the law that had been responsible for supporting injustices, while operating against "good will" themselves. In reality, supporting and obeying the law in this circumstance would be equivalent to aiding and strengthening one's oppressor; or supporting and conspiring with murderers and organized criminals. However, this is her idea of being a good Christian.

STEALTH

Other than discouraging people to oppose oppressive and racist powers, Christianity has encouraged people to be subservient in numerous ways that may not be obvious to the average person. Considering that we live in modern times, conventional and traditional ways of living have become obsolete. Early settlers used horses and wagons for transportation until the invention of the automobile and airplane. Even airplanes have evolved to become more efficient. During World Wars I and II, airplanes were very effective for transportation and air attacks. However, technology improved and radar was introduced, making aircraft detectable and vulnerable to enemy fire. As a result, stealth bombers were introduced to fly over hostile territories because they could not be detected by radar. Stealth allowed this new form of aircraft to conduct military operations that more traditional aircraft could not.

When people can detect and recognize a problem they have a better chance of solving or overcoming it. Because racism and oppression were so blatant and obvious in the form of black slavery, Jim Crow laws, and segregation, they had to evolve into new forms that would be less detectable in order to exist in a more advanced society. Today no one is going to say, "Hey you with the big lips and nappy hair. I'm a racist. I'm not going to hire you because I discriminate against your people." It doesn't work like that.

INSTITUTIONAL RACISM

Individual racism is not as serious as it used to be, considering that segregation mainly exists covertly, and it is now possible to sue for racial discrimination is some instances. The real problem today is institutional racism: legislative laws, practices, and policies of corporations, universities and other institutions that affect the foundation we stand on. The passing of the Civil Rights Amendment of 1967 did make changes in terms of segregation; however, when we look at the low quality of healthcare, education, and adequate legal representation that minorities still receive and the large economic gap between them and whites, we can see that very little has changed. It is as if we are living in a "desegregated" pre-civil rights era.

Segregation was, and still is, implemented to make a systematic way of making sure that not everyone receives the same privileges. Because it's centuries old enforcement has only ended a short period ago, its affects are still felt and practiced today. Much of it is a result of abolished laws that have paved the path for a segregationist culture that still exists.

For example, people were arrested for even intermarrying across racial lines in seventeen states until the latter part of the twentieth century—all of them located in the "Bible belt." [2]

The 1967 decision of *Loving v. Virginia* finally allowed whites and others to marry. However, the South still remains segregated well into the new millennium.

The *Loving v. Virginia* case began when a white man, Richard Loving, and a black woman, Mildred Jeter, were married in the District of Columbia in June 1958. They returned to Virginia and lived together in Caroline County. They were arrested for violating Virginia's ban of interracial Marriage. They pleaded guilty to the charges on January 6, 1959 and were sentenced to one year in jail. The trial judge gave them a suspended sentence for a period of 25 years on the condition that the Lovings leave the state and not return for 25 years. The Chief Justice Warren delivered the following opinion in court:

> "Almighty God created the races white, black, yellow, malay and red, and he placed them on separate continents. And but for the interference with this arrangement there would be no cause for such marriages. The fact that he separated the races shows that he did not intend for the races to mix."[12]

Although this happened in 1967, segregation is still strong in the south, and the American criminal and political systems are still run by those who make decisions that are severely crippling to minorities. Their effects can be seen in the hundreds of inner-city ghettos that exist all across the map. They determine what race of people get city, state, and federal contracts for construction and hundreds of other fields as well as what districts receive better education and other provisions.

George Allen, former governor (1994-1998) and senator (2000-2006) of Virginia, was often criticized for making policies and passing laws that were anti-minority oriented: he abolished parole, dramatically reduced the

---

2   The seventeen states were: Alabama, Arkansas, Delaware, Florida, Georgia, Kentucky, Louisiana, Maryland, Mississippi, Missouri, North Carolina, Oklahoma, South Carolina, Tennessee, Texas, Virginia, and West Virginia

amount of good time prisoners could earn, and reduced funds for educational programs that would have actually contributed in reducing crime. Many people argued that he was not a racist at that time, nor were his policies. He went on to become Senator for the state, bringing his policies with him.

During a videotaped interview on "August 11, 2006, George Allen is shown taunting a dark skinned American citizen of Indian descent. The man, S.R. Sidharth, 20, a University of Virginia student, was campaigning for Allen's opponent, Jim Web, at the time. Allen is taped saying, "This fellow here, over here with the yellow shirt, *macaca*, or whatever his name is. He's with my opponent. Let's give a welcome to *macaca*, here. Welcome to America."[13]

Despite the fact that the man was born in Fairfax, Virginia, the Senator's attitude showed that he felt that only "pink" complexioned people have the right to call themselves Americans, and even human, considering that a macaca is a species of monkey. The term is used in Africa where people believe that Allen learned the term from his mother who is a Jew of Tunisian descent.

The *New Republic* reported that Allen wore a Confederate flag pin in high school year book photo; had a Confederate flag placed on his car; had Confederate flags at his house as well as his house for his first campaign ad for governor in 1993. On September 24, 2006, *Salon* online magazine reported that three college football teammates said that Allen used racial epithets to refer to blacks and even went as far a putting a deer head in the mailbox of a black family.

After George Allen's racist statements, the *USA Today* interviewed two white women named Pat Harrington and Delrose Winter about their position on Allen. Harrington, who is a part-time real estate agent, a resident of Leesburg, VA said, "He's a wonderful man. A good Christian."[14] She later vowed to vote for Allen in the upcoming elections.

THE POWER OF MINORITY LEADERS?

Although there have been, and are, people of color in power, such as Chief Justice, Clarence Thomas; former Secretary of State, Condoleezza Rice; and

Attorney General, Alberto Gonzalez, and President Barak Obama, they served solely as providing minority visibility. Their decisions have made little, if any, improvements to those groups from which they have come from.

In fact, minorities are often used to orchestrate certain types of discrimination in order to camouflage the culprit and shift the blame to someone just happy to have a position. This is the real problem with institutional racism: the culprit is hidden, and no one knows who to blame because it appears to be a system that is inclusive to everyone. We may go into a bank and see racial diversity amongst the tellers and managers, but when we look at the bank's policies we can see a lack of equality as reported by Robert Wesley in *Many Billions Gone, The Boston College Law Review* (1999):

> Based on discrimination in home mortgage approval rates the projected number of credit-worthy home buyers and the median white housing appreciation rate, it is estimated that the current generation of blacks will lose about $82 billion in equity due to institutional discrimination. All things being equal, the next generation of blacks will lose about $93 billion.
> As the cardinal means of middle class wealth accumulation, the missed opportunity for home equity due to private and governmental racial discrimination is devastating to the black community."[15]

PRISON OR SLAVERY?

After slavery was abolished in America, the plantation was replaced by the penitentiary. Although slavery was abolished, it was—and still is—prescribed as a punishment for anyone convicted of a crime, as mentioned in the Thirteenth Amendment of the Constitution of the United States of America: "[Slavery Prohibited] Neither slavery nor involuntary servitude, except as a punishment for crime whereof the party shall have been duly convicted, shall exist within the United States, or any place subject to their jurisdiction (Article XIII—section I). Although many have tried to define slavery as being an institution of the past, international law defines "slavery" as being any form of "forced labor":

On July 2, 1998, the Commission issued its report. This report acknowledges that the definition of slavery has historically been a narrow one, but then states that the term "slavery" now encompasses forced labor.

In international law, the prohibition of recourse to forced labour has its origin in the efforts made by the international community to eradicate slavery, its institutions and similar practices, since forced labour is considered to be one of these slavery-like practices....Although certain instruments, and particularly those adopted at the beginning of the nineteenth century, define slavery in a restrictive manner, the prohibition of slavery must now be understood as covering all contemporary manifestations of this practice.[16]

After the abolishment of slavery, blacks were once again subject to performing free labor through being incarcerated. Even today, they are racially profiled as being criminals and targeted more frequently by the law than white Americans. It was the Thirteenth Amendment that has acted as a Covenant between man and man, to sanction the enslavement of human beings. It sanctioned slavery as a punishment to the offender, while neglecting to place an emphasis on compensation to the victim of the offense. Because minorities are often the victims of this law, its application is almost identical to how the Bible has prescribed servitude to the descendants of Ham as punishment. Looking at the disproportionately large amount of minorities that are incarcerated and forced into performing labor for slave wages, often as low as twenty cents per hour, we have a right to the claim that the Christian founders of America were inspired by the Bible to form a Covenant of their own that could justify forced labor of African Americans and other peoples of color.

Just like the waging of war, incarceration begins with a claim that someone has done something wrong. However, fraudulent charges and long sentences that do not reflect the nature of the offenses are often issued to African Americans so that slave labor can be provided for the federal and state governments and to their private investors and associates. By 2004, government reports showed that over 60 percent of prison and jail inmates were of ethnic or racial minorities. An alarming 12.6 percent of all black men in their upper 20s were incarcerated, opposed to 3.6 percent of Hispanic men and 1.7 percent of white men in the same age group.

Prison being a replacement of slavery is not a claim supported only by minorities in America, but by many whites as well. Molly Secours, a *white* freelance journalist and film producer has documented the effects of racism on a global level. She has produced numerous works on the subject of white privilege and its consequences for both victim and perpetrator. She was also a delegate to the *2001 United Nations World Conference Against Racism in South Africa*. In her report titled *Riding the Reparations Bandwagon* she states:

> ….When we look at the figures of who is in prison and we realize that there were few prisons in America during slavery, we must ask unthinkable questions. Why are American prisons one of the fastest-growing businesses in this country? Why are they being privatized? Has our prison system replaced slavery? Is it possible that black men and women are deemed less threatening to whites when they are held captive in controlled environments? Does the justice system reflect an unconscious conviction of white society, that prison is where people of color belong? Have we returned to the era of "convict leasing" as recently reported by Doug Blackmon in the *Wall Street Journal*, when African American prisoners were leased to private corporations? All of these complicated questions are relevant to the issue of reparations and deserve to be answered honestly and objectively.[17]

WHO IS THE LAW FOR?

Although minorities have not been proven to be more prone to criminal activity than whites genetically, minorities overpopulate the prison system because tougher laws are passed against crimes that are more common in minority communities such as drug and gun offenses.

If we reflect back to the booming drug trade of the inner-cities during the nineteen eighties and early nineties, we'll notice a dramatic increase in the amount of prisoners from minority groups following the government's war on drugs. Although selling drugs is not a legitimate profession, it is no more severe than other crimes committed. Despite that drug dealing is a non-violent crime; many drug dealers get more time in prison than rapists and murderers.

Just to confirm that these laws were applied discriminately, after two decades of debating, in 2007 the United States Sentencing Commission reduced the sentencing guidelines for crack cocaine offenses and recommended that Congress address the long mandatory minimum sentences pertaining to low level crack offenses. Newscasters spoke of a crack "epidemic" and "crisis" in the eighties which frightened many people, including those who live in crack infested neighborhoods that had not seen much of a crisis except for young black males flashing money and walking around wearing big gold chains.

Critics say that these laws were passed due to public demand. Well, if public demand really influences laws, then why aren't stricter laws passed against corporate criminals and crystal meth drug users and dealers, considering that the public is screaming for a reform that would give them longer sentences? Could it be that these types of crimes would most likely effect white America more than anyone else? It is evident that the judicial system and other social institutions of today are actually extensions of a post slavery plan that was well documented in W.E.B. Dubois' *Souls of Black Folks* (1903):

> ....the passing of a great human institution before its work is done, like the untimely passing of a single soul, but leaves a legacy of striving for other men. The legacy of the Freedmen's Bureau is the heavy heritage of this generation. Today, when new and vaster problems are destined to strain every fiber of the national mind and soul, would it not be well to count this legacy honestly and carefully? For this much all men know: despite compromise, war, and struggle, the Negro is not free. In the Backwoods of the Gulf States, for miles and miles, he may not leave the plantation of his birth; in well-nigh the whole rural south the black farmers are peons, bound by law and custom to an economic slavery, from which the only escape is death or the penitentiary. In the most cultured sections and cities of the South the Negroes are a segregated servile caste. Before the courts, both in law and custom, they stand on a different and peculiar basis. Taxation without representation is the rule of their political life. And the result of all this is, and in nature must have been, lawlessness and crime. That is the large legacy of the Freedmen's Bureau, the work it did not do because it could not.[18]

CRIMINALIZATION

Through many years of criminalization, an American culture has evolved that sanctions crime as a key element to African American culture. This element of crime is often the trap that snares people of color into situations of servitude, which is often justified by the claim that "the law was broken." However, this element of crime is actually marketed and publicly sanctioned to minorities.

Perhaps there is a movie that shows a person behaving in a certain way and doing things that bring about successful results; whether the actor's behavior in the movie was good or bad, the viewer may imitate that individual in real life, with the intention of obtaining success through using the same tactics. Entertainers often portray certain groups, races, or religions in positive or negative ways. The audience may accept what has been portrayed as being reality. If so, they may then be influenced to believe that the lifestyles and decisions of these entertainers are socially acceptable and mandated by society as being the absolute e standard one should try to follow. This encourages the audience to uphold and support these stereotypical standards of living and behavioral patterns in their everyday lives.

There is a very popular sit-com called *The Fresh Prince of Bellaire*. In the show, Will Smith is a young hip-hop styled young man, who leaves the ghetto of West Philadelphia to stay with his Aunt Vivian and Uncle Phil in their mansion in Bellaire, California. Will is portrayed as being a wise-cracking silly young man, who uses his hip-hop style of slang, street wit, and sarcasm to navigate his way throughout everyday life amongst the elite, obtain respect, make dates with beautiful girls, and obtain success in school. His best friend is an African American young man named Jazz. He is portrayed as a reprobate, who earns his livelihood through different schemes based on dishonesty and trickery, with overwhelmingly successful results.

Amongst the other characters is Will's Uncle Phil, his cousin, Carlton, and the black butler, Jeffrey. Despite the Uncle Phil is a well-educated judge; he is portrayed as a fat, baldheaded mini-tyrant who is vilified through the extreme sternness that he shows towards Will and his own children. Carlton's elite education and superb etiquette is dwarfed and negated by his inability to obtain social acceptance and respect from Will—as well as from the other characters on the show. Then there is the most articulate of them all—Jeffrey—the butler.

Shows like these are extremely influential on society because they are targeted for young people. They give young people examples of what types of behavior and tactics will bring them power, respect, social acceptance, and success. For the young mind that has not yet established values and opinions, it is more than likely that they will use Will Smith and his degenerate friend Jazz as models to follow to obtain respect, social acceptance, power, and success.

Children learn from the most influential things in their environment. In many cases, they are influenced by things that do not have their best interest in mind. Consequently, they tend to carry their childhood beliefs, attitudes, and experiences with them throughout their adult lives—which explains many of the social ills that western societies now face: gangs, crime, as well as a new breed of delinquent and violent youth.

It's not a crime to follow the hip hop culture; however, it is an injustice to tell young African Americans that educating themselves will abase them to servants, as in the case of Jeffrey, the articulate black butler. Nor will an education make them fat, baldheaded mini-tyrants like Uncle Phil, or unpopular, egotistical, Uncle Toms as portrayed by Will's cousin, Carlton.

In reality, an education *will* contribute to one's success in the real world, in one way or another; whereas, acting foolishly and using street corner tactics to maneuver one throughout life is useless. The "Fresh-Prince-scenario" is just a random example of the many thorns in minority success that exist in the entertainment world. There are a disproportionately large amount of songs, videos, and movies that show minorities living luxurious lifestyles, surrounded by envious people: results of criminal activities and unorthodox street tactics, rather than through the use of morality and education. Crime and corruption are often the sources of success. The young people who are parented by the entertainment world may be influenced to support and uphold what has been sanctioned acceptable by these entertainers as "norms of society", or the society that they belong to. These well-edited and thoroughly rehearsed forms of entertainment are often extremely appealing and influential to young people. They usually vilify morality and education and glamorize corruption and the street life. The entertainment world acts as baby sitters for most children and raises them to become adults in the light of whatever has been the most influential and dominant messages.

It is not only racial profiling and the vilification of minority groups that puts them in situations such as prisons, where they can be exploited and oppressed, forced into doing free labor. Moreover, it is the publicly sanctioned idea by Judeo-Christian America that being a criminal is often the "black thing to do"; just as obtaining an education is often portrayed as being the "white thing to do". We can conclude that this is why many minorities are discouraged from obtaining an education. They have been taught to believe that reaching high standards of morality and education would be a deviation from their culture, which has led to an entire segment of society fulfilling subservient roles. This is not some abstract idea, considering that it is the nature of human beings to become swept up in the avalanche of whatever cultural practices are common.

Through the Communications Act of 1934, it is the responsibility of the government to make sure that what is published or broadcasted does not harm public interest. The Federal Communications Committee (FCC) is authorized to make rules and regulations that can prohibit the publication and broadcasting of certain material that may harm public interest. However, it seems as though the public interest of Judeo-Christian America is to allow the broadcasting and publication of material that is subversive to the social and intellectual development of people as long as it is marketed to people of African and other non-European descent: Hispanics, Asians, and even some Europeans such as Italians (who have enough melanin in their skin and curl in their hair to be labeled as murderous, Mafia-affiliated mulattos).

It is not the blame of either white or non-white America that there are more negative images of minorities that often undermine their development. It is a collective effort of all of Judeo-Christian America that allows this injustice to occur. The leaders write the script as the masses follow obediently. All have the ability to stop it in the name of the religions that they follow; however, it seems as though it is their religious beliefs that often provide the premises that are used to justify the subservience of African and other non-white peoples.

No matter how many may wish to dispute this idea, certain facts remain true; most importantly, the fact that Fox, Paramount MGM, Universal

Pictures, and Warner Brothers were all started by Jewish businessmen in the early part of the twentieth century. They are still owned and operated by a vast amount of Jews whose numbers are much higher than the percentage that exists in the national population. This also holds true for almost every major media and music company, as well as their distribution outlets. Whether one is talking about Spielberg or Rick Ruben (movie producer and founder of Def Jam), the majority of the "shot callers" are Jews, and many even Zionists (not only by name). LL Cool J expressed this correctly on his song *I Can't Live Without My Radio*: "I'm good to go on your radio, and cold gettin' paid 'cause Rick said so!"

Therefore, it is more than just a coincidence that the book they (Jews and Christians) happen to look towards for guidance designates servitude for people of African descent as well s the music and movies that they produce. From the beginning, the Bible has not been about the elimination of African peoples, but controlling them and making sure that they are in subservient positions. The entertainment world and the media are the most influential tools in orchestrating racial opinions and attitudes.

Although I've just briefly summarized the blueprint of "how" the ancient Biblical teachings of African subservience is molded into today's world, we still have to analyze the deeper, more catastrophic circumstances of how "people" have been effected by the criminal justice system which has now spread far beyond race, as well as the stealth of institutional racism. To truly understand contemporary oppression we have to analyze the lifelong shackle of felony disenfranchisement, its consequences, and the danger that lies within the facade of its innocent appearance and justified existence.

CHAPTER 3

You Better Recognize:
the stealth of institutional racism

In order to overcome something we have understand its existence and how it operates. Out of the nearly five hundred people that I interviewed to gather information on this material, almost all of the immigrant Muslims that I spoke to, that grew up in Muslim countries, did not admit to facing any racism either in their native countries or in America, whereas, most Muslims from Western nations such as France, England, and the United States admitted that it existed in their countries, even if they had parents that were from Muslim countries. I attribute this to the following facts concerning Muslims that grew up in Islamic countries that I interviewed:

1) They did not perceive racism because they were not racists. They viewed others as they saw life—fair—known as "projection" in psychology.

2) They judged the fairness of the United States by their own personal economic success, comparing it to how financially well off they were in their former countries. Often an improvement of their personal living conditions gave them a certain contentment that made them overlook the social and economic inequalities that existed amongst the American population.

3) They were business owners or professionals (doctors) and were financially stable and never placed in vulnerable situations where the affairs of their lives were in the hands of the "system": police brutality that many

face in ghettos, correction officers, judges, prosecutors, case workers, parole boards, employers of menial jobs, and others who tend to have a disdain for the poor, who usually view them as a strain on society's resources.

4) They did not have any negative stereotypes that followed them as African Americans and Latinos do, so they couldn't feel what others experienced. They were looked at as a "resume" or a potential employee rather than a threat on job interviews. Even African immigrants were referred to as Somalis or Egyptians rather than "black" (descendants of slaves) despite that there may have not been any physical difference between them and American born African Americans. Therefore, they were not included within the American racial caste system because they had no place.

5) They did not *recognize* racism or discrimination when it existed; whereas, Muslims native to the United States (including those with immigrant parents) where more familiar with discriminatory colloquial expressions and customs that were very subtle, but whose effects were very severe.

For example, when I asked the question "If there is anything in America that you could change, what would it be?" almost all of them said, "The way the media portrays Muslims."

Although they agreed that the Muslims were being stereotyped, they couldn't piece together that Arabs, Pakistanis, Egyptians, Afghans, and other "brown" peoples were the victims of this distortion of character, which is crippling to their forward progression, while "pink" colored people were not. They also did not understand that the negative images of African Americans were just as much disliked by African Americans in the United States who also perceived it as being a misrepresentation of who they were.

Most immigrants I interviewed were educated and understood English from an academic approach, unaware of the meanings of many euphemisms and behaviors used in casual conversations that, as in all cultures, take a life time to understand. For example, In California, police jargon and terms such as NHI (No Humans Involved) are sometimes used by police officers in reference to low priority homicide cases that involve minorities, prostitutes, and lower class whites, where there is not much emphasis placed on response time or investigative thoroughness.[1] There are acronyms such as "UNIT" that many may interpret as being either part of a complex whole or an individual thing regarded for purposes of calculation, but has actually been used by police in upstate New York to indicate an "Unwanted Nigger In Town".[2]

Even some African American Muslims, at times, did not realize that they were being discriminated against until it was actually brought to their attention. One Muslim man, Kyle Burton (Kamal), who was the first African American fireman to walk into his predominantly Irish firehouse in Flatbush, Brooklyn in thirty years, noticed that white colleagues would wipe their hands off after they would shake his hand when he would visit other firehouses;[*] whereas, the black ones would give him the "ghetto handshake" with a chest bump and hug.[3]

INSTITUIONAL RACISM

When we talk about racism we want to talk about racism that is effective. I'm not dealing with someone rolling their eyes at you, or failing to greet you. We see interracial couples and interactions all the time. Racism that doesn't affect your quality of life or "pockets" is not worth mentioning to most people. *Institutional* and *not* individual racism is what is up for discussion. Institutional racism is the most dangerous and subtle form, because it appears as though certain laws and policies exist as affecting all of society instead of just one particular group. Moreover, there is no clear cut culprit to blame, because it "seems" as though it is a law or policy that was implemented by society to benefit all citizens.

In France, Muslim women began to dominate the medical fields. As a response, laws prohibiting women from wearing the hijab were passed. Women were also forced to practice medicine on both men and women. This seemed like a fair law because it was for all women. However, white French women were not affected because covering their hair and not touching men is not an integral part of Christianity. Therefore, this was a tactic used to prohibit Middle Eastern and African women (who are primarily

---

* This is something that psychologists have recorded by racists who say that they often feel "squeamish" when shaking hands with someone of another race. Daniel Goldman, Interview with Thomas Pettigrew: *The New York Times* (Aug. 26, 1990)

Muslim) from participating in the medical field. People in France are also prohibited from wearing anything that reflects any religious or political affiliation in school. Since French political parties or being a Christian doesn't require you to wear any special type of clothing, the only people affected are Muslim women who can't wear their hijab.

The same holds true for Palestinian students who seek higher education to combat Israeli aggression. In places like the city of Qalqilyah, which is surrounded by a wall, there is only one gate that allows exit and entry to Al-Quds University for "security" reasons; enrollment has grown enormously. [4]Dr. Attia Muslah, head of the local branch reported to the *Israeli daily Ha'aretz* on July 30, 2004, "Most of our students are people who work or have worked—farmers, teachers, businessmen. Some of them lost their lands or their ability to work them as a result of the construction of the wall. Others lost their jobs. People today prefer to scrimp on bread, and invest in attaining education, out of recognition of the social value of attaining education in Palestinian society. They also know that the knowledge they attain cannot be taken away from them."[5] Despite the Palestinians efforts, the Israeli military continuously tries to prohibit the Palestinians, not Israelis, from crossing roadblocks for "security" reasons where Jews are not affected. When these policies are pushed in the name of security it makes them appear justifiable to the world, when in reality, it's a racist policy that only attacks those of the bloodline of Ishmael (Palestinians).

SUCCESS

Moreover, as I did my investigation on the success of the individuals I interviewed, *all* of them attributed their success to the economic and emotional support and ethical guidance that their families and communities had given them. The fact that no one did it alone was evidence that communal success was directly related to individual success. The destruction or "obstruction" of a community's success usual determines the opportunities and the percentage of a chance that the individual will succeed, unless that person is that one out of a thousand. Through a systematic scheme implemented by powerful people, well-educated in social sciences, criminology, and business, communal success has been easily manipulated in the U.S. in terms of who will and will not have "individual" success.

FELONY DISENFRANCHISEMENT

The two most oppressive elements that exist today are incarceration and felony disenfranchisement. Felony disenfranchisement can be traced back to the ancient Greeks, where a serious crime outside of their social norms allowed an individual to be declared socially dead. He or she could not vote, appear in court, make speeches, attend assemblies, serve in the army, or participate in politics.[6] At that time there were blacks from Ethiopia in Greece; however, their participation in society was limited to military service, slavery, or trading exotic things such as elephant tusks and perfumes. They were socially dead just as Africans are dead in modern societies of Greek influence (America) through laws and policies that systematically kill their participation in fields that significantly impact society. In fact, the word nekros is the root of the word "negro" or "black" which itself means dead. From an apparently primary nekus (a corpse); dead (literally or figuratively; also as noun) -- dead. [7]

Today, the U.S. disenfranchises more people than any other nation in the world.[7] There is an estimated 4.7 million Americans that cannot obtain descent employment or vote because of their criminal records,[8] which includes roughly 600,000 veterans; by 2000, an estimated 1.6 million of them had served all of their time and were no longer under federal or state supervision.[9] As we look closer we see that the racial differences in the segment of that population are astounding. About 1.4 million African American males are among the 4.7 million disenfranchised Americans, which is about 30% of the total.[10] What is shocking is that African American males only make up 6.2% of the U.S. Population.[11] At this current rate, 40% of the present generation of African American males can expect to be disenfranchised citizens at some point of their lives.

WHY DO THESE NUMBERS EXIST?

Causes of crimes are generally categorized into three main groups by criminologists: economic factors/poverty, social environment, and family structures.[12] However, these are more or less circumstances forced on to African Americans through centuries of slavery, segregation, and other demoralizing living conditions rather than a blatant disregard for the law, or selecting a reprobate lifestyle over capitalizing off of an abundance of economic opportunities. Furthermore, the real underlying reason of such a high incarceration and disenfranchisement rate amongst African Americans is that tougher laws are passed for crimes common in African American communities—institutional racism.

Being caught in the web of the criminal justice system makes it "appear" as though the harsh sentences are justifiable on the premise that "someone broke the law." However, there is no such thing as a crime free ethnic group in the United States. Certain crimes are more common within certain areas or ethnic groups due to availability to the means to orchestrate a particular crime, and generally, information on how to commit it are often shared within tight nit communities.

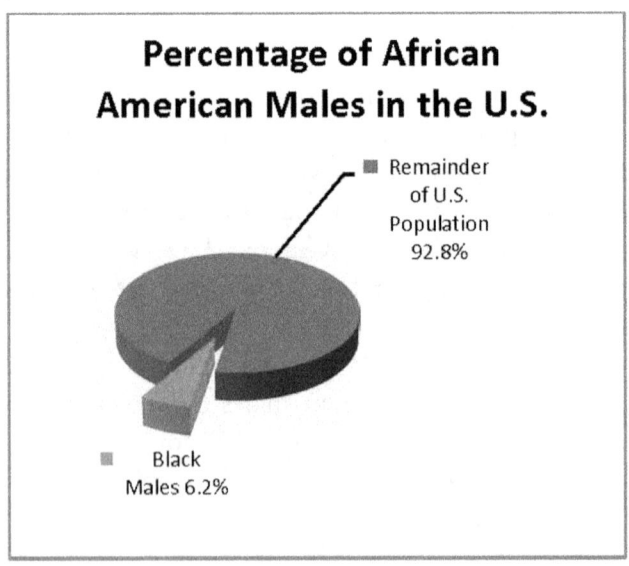

SOURCE: *U.S. Census Bureau, Race Alone or in Combination: 2000*

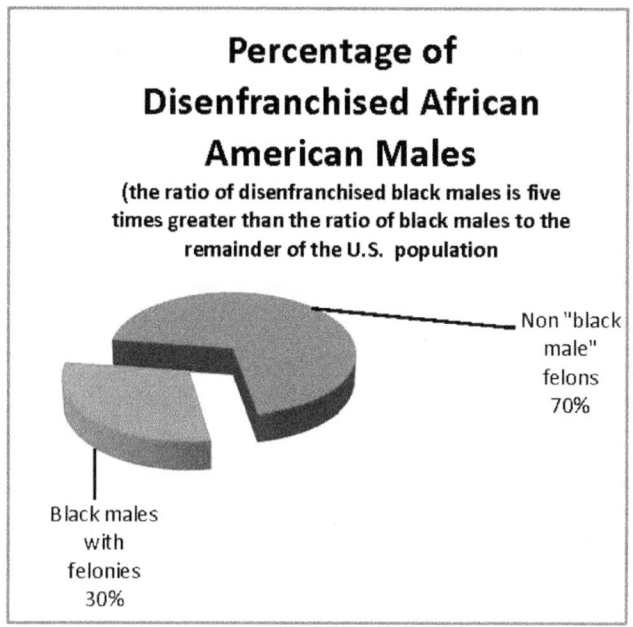

SOURCE: *The Sentencing Project, supra note 115*

For example, crystal meth is a drug common in white rural communities. A 2005 report stated that in North Dakota alone, a predominantly white state, 60% of the male prison population was meth users, while 80-90% of the female population was incarcerated for meth related offenses.[13] However, meth users and dealers are often treated as victims in the criminal justice system, where they undertake drug treatment programs instead of long prison sentences that are given to African Americans who are convicted of selling crack cocaine.

A lot of people asked me how I could discuss drugs so freely in a book that is about Quranic solutions to overcome racism and oppression. My answer is simple: Islam is based on the truth and the realities of man. Just as the image of a child being buried alive is offensive to most people, the Prophet Muhammad (ص) would speak about it freely because it was part of the dark realities that the Arabs faced at that time. It is also mentioned in the Quran in several places.

---

* See photo of Wood Harris, Mekhi Phifer, and Cameron Giles.

Likewise, drug abuse is a major problem in the United States, and almost everyone is affected by it directly or indirectly: taxpayers, those who have family members addicted to drugs or in prison for selling them, business owners who have losses from those that steal for drugs, etc. Even the people that have the most trustworthy positions in society have used drugs, which include presidents Obama, Clinton, and Bush.

Obama admitted it openly;[14] Bush had a possession of cocaine charge expunged from his record in 1972,[15] while it is widely known within Bill Clinton's social circles that he was a "recreational" cocaine user, [16] not to mention that he admitted to smoking, but not inhaling marijuana. Many others in prominent circles also used the drug which was quite expensive until the 1980s.

THE CRACK WAVE AND WHY IT WAS POPULAR IN AFRICAN AMERICAN COMMUNITIES

Crack appeared in the 1980's as an affordable form of cocaine because dealers learned to "fluff up" the drug by mixing it with other things. Both powder and crack cocaine puts the user on a "chase", where he or she will continuously try to recapture the stimulus of the original dosage that would last only five to ten minutes. However, the duration of each additional "high" lasts less than the original. Therefore, it was a quick "hustle" for many black males, serving as an immediate remedy for those who faced job discrimination and saw no long term solution for the socio-economic obstacles that they faced as minorities.

Furthermore, the demographical make up of minority communities made the trade more logical to take place there because drug use is a coping strategy for their stressful living conditions. It is also normal for urban areas where people live crammed in tenements and high rise apartments that have high unemployment rates to have above average pedestrian traffic and loitering. Therefore, drug traffic blended in easier there where it was hard to distinguish between a dealer, user, or resident. Most urban areas during the 1980's were filled with poorly educated economically depressed youth that often believed that they could escape the ghetto by selling drugs. Also, the almost suicidal "don't-care-attitude" is common in urban areas as a tactic to cope with certain harsh realities as violence and economic hopelessness. Life in the drug game was considered just as risky as walking home from school, but paying a whole lot more.

The educational system was also a great factor in the growth of the drug trade. Instead of teaching about the Moors in Spain and other African empires and contributions, it taught that from the beginning of their existence in the United States, African Americans were slaves, marginalized from the rest of society, which is not much different than being a drug dealer. Secondly, it taught bland memorization of dates, historical events, and arithmetic tables, but suffered from convenient amnesia when it was time to teach them that they could never use what they had learned if they were convicted of a felony.

Figure 1: Race/Ethnicity of Cocaine Defendants

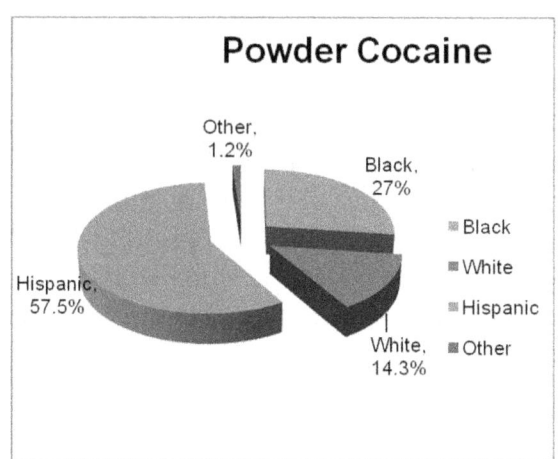

SOURCE: *U.S. Sentencing Commission, 2005 Drug Sample.*

Figure 1: Race/Ethnicity of Crack Cocaine Defendants

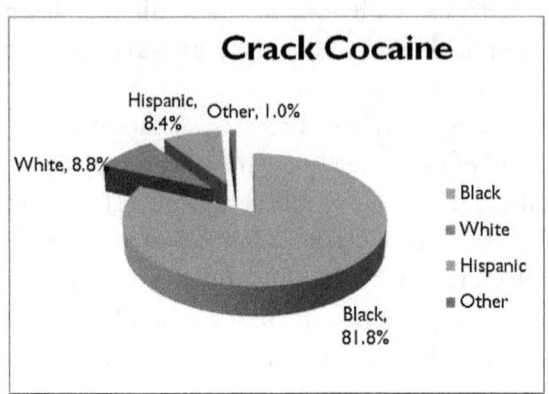

SOURCE: U.S. Sentencing Commission, 2005 Drug Sample

THE MEDIA

Newscasters used words such as "plague", "epidemic", and "crisis" to describe the new trade during the eighties to frighten citizens into supporting the Reagan administration's War on Drugs. However, a recent medical review of the so-called "catastrophic" effects of the drug shows that the only crisis was that young black males wear sporting gold chains and flashing large amounts of money as they drove around in new cars fresh out the showroom with sayings like "How you like me now!" stenciled in calligraphy along the sides.

CRACK MYTHS

Violence
The violence involved with the crack trade made many believe that it was a result of the physiological effects of the drug. However, in its May 2002 recommendations to Congress, the U.S. Sentencing Commission stated that the crack penalties were based on "beliefs" about the drug's association with violence which had been proven to be inaccurate. Its 2007 report stated a decline

in associated violence (bodily injury or threats) for crack and powder cocaine charges.[17] The Sentencing Commission concluded that the violence associated with crack is primarily related to the drug trade and not any effects of the drug itself, and that both powder and crack cocaine cause distribution-related violence, as do all drug markets. This was a result of rival dealers disputing over territories, and often being targeted by robbers who perceived them as easy prey simply because they had to keep a low profile and could not report their losses to the police.* There were still other cases were crack users were victims of violence by young people who deemed them as being weak and vulnerable. In a review of federal cases for 2005, the Sentencing Commission reported that a majority of crack cocaine cases (67.6%) and powder cocaine cases (84.3%) did not include an offender who "had access to, possession of, or used a weapon"; indeed, the frequency with which weapons are used by the offender is extremely low, 0.8% of powder cases and 2.9% of crack cases.[1]

Crack Baby
The media also drilled the illusion of the "crack baby" to champion a sympathetic following of citizens to combat their fictitious war on drugs. The media would often show premature babies crying and trembling from what they described as withdrawal symptoms of crack. However, after years of reviewing, the medical field concluded that the effects of crack on a fetus had been overstated.[20] Deborah Frank, a professor of Pediatrics at Boston University describes the "crack baby" as "a grotesque media stereotype, not a scientific diagnosis."[21] She also discovered that the negative effects of crack use on the fetus are similar to the negative effects of tobacco or alcohol use, poor prenatal care or poor nutrition of the fetus.

Addictiveness
Many studies show that the physiological and psychotropic effects of crack and powder are the same; the drugs are now widely acknowledged as pharmacologically identical. A 1996 study published in the *Journal of the American Medical Association* finds identical effects on the body for both crack and powder cocaine.[22] Charles Schuster, former Director of the National Institute on Drug Abuse and Professor of Psychiatry and Behavioral

---

*   See photo of Wood Harris, Mekhi Phifer, and Cameron Giles.

Sciences, recognized that when cocaine is absorbed into the bloodstream and gets to the brain its effects on brain chemistry are one and the same despite whether it is crack or powder.[23]

DRUG QUANTITIES AND CRACK COCAINE PENALTIES

Congress "openly" proposed the logical solution by passing laws that "would" target the source of the drug trade: cut the root and the tree will fall. Eliminate high-level drug market operators (manufacturers or heads of organizations distributing commercial amounts of narcotics and other *serious* trackers) and then it will be eliminated on a consumer level.[24] It sounded great to many citizens and law makers; however, when the federal sentencing laws were passed by Congress in the 1980s it was a leaf plucking process that targeted street-level African American drug dealers and did nothing to eliminate drug trafficking. However, the Sentencing Commission testified that the five grams that Congress proposed to trigger the mandatory five year minimum was an amount considered small for even low-level dealers, not close to mid-level, and not within an eye reach of the intended target—high-level dealers.[25] Only 52 grams of crack called for a mandatory of ten years in federal court, where 340 grams of powder cocaine did not even call for five years. Therefore, the Commission ruled that more low-level dealers are filling the system that have very little responsibility for drug trafficking.[26]

THE EFFECTS ON AFRICAN AMERICANS

African American drug defendants have a 20 percent more likely of being sentenced to prison than white drug defendants.[28] From 1994 until 2003, the average sentence served by African Americans for drug offenses increased by 62 percent, compared to an increase of only 17 percent for whites convicted of the same crimes.[29] African Americans now serve practically as much time in prison for drugs (58.7 months) as whites do for violent crimes (61.7 months).[30] Therefore, the Sentencing Commission reported in 2004 that "[r]evising the crack cocaine thresholds would better reduce the [sentencing] gap than any other single policy change, and it would dramatically improve the fairness of the federal sentencing system."³¹

This decision seemed to be a victory for many in the African American communities, but after two decades of children growing up without their incarcerated parents, communities without authoritative male role models, and the psychological and emotional effects on blacks that served astronomically longer sentences than whites, it will take several generations to reverse these affects of these biased government decisions.

(Courtesy of Roc-A-Fella Films)
The film 'paid in full' starring Wood Harris, Mekhi Phifer, and Cameron Giles was based off of the screen play Trapped of Azie Faison, Jr., a Harlem drug dealer who barely survived a shooting in the nineteen eighties. Trapped was what Faison referred to as the black Titanic. Phifer was killed in a robbery and Harris (portraying) Faison was also shot in the head in a robbery attempt. Paid in Full was a graphic film that captured factual elements of the street life: the quick dollar as a solution to a dead end job, the overnight black wealth that made much of America squeamish with envy, the respect and love obtained from money, and not to mention betrayal.

Figure 1: Cocaine Sentences for Quantities Less Than 25 Grams

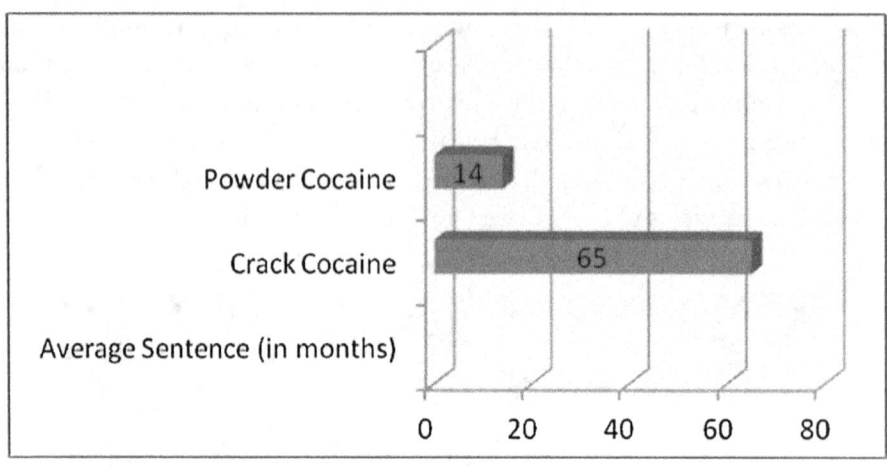

Source: U.S. Department of Justice, <u>Federal Cocaine Offenses: An Analysis of Crack and Powder Penalties</u>, March 17, 2002.

Table 1: Median Street Level Dealer Drug Quantities and Mandatory Minimums

Drug	Median Drug Weight	Applicable Mandatory Minimum
Crack Cocaine	52 Grams	10 Years
Powder Cocaine	340 Grams	none

Figure: Defendant Function in Crack/Powder Cocaine Cases (who goes to prison)

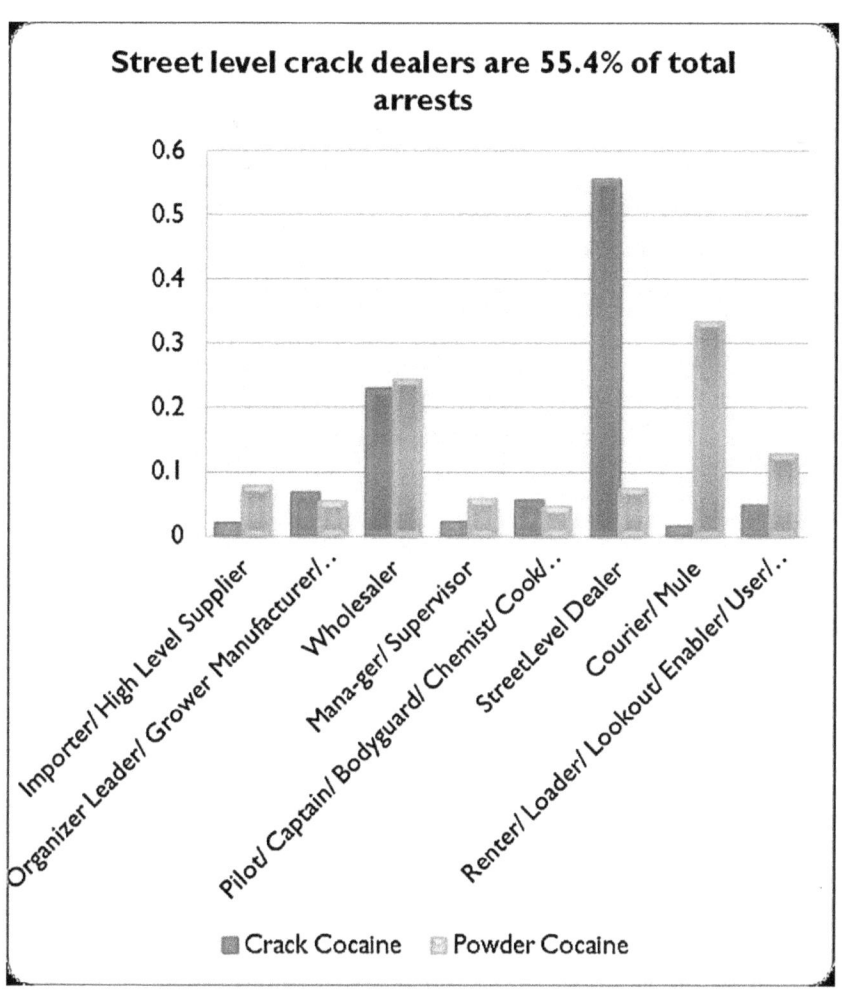

SOURCE: *U.S. Sentencing Commission, 2005 Drug Sample*

Just because the sentencing guidelines were changed does not mean that justice was served. Authorities replaced the unjust sentencing guidelines with eliminating federal assistance to drug offenders, while no restrictions apply to violent offenders such as murderers and child molesters.

According to Justice Department statistics, white inmates were nearly three times more likely to have victimized a child than black inmates,[31] and most child molesters in general are white males,[32] but upon release, they qualify for financial aid and other government services restricted from drug offenders.

Benefit	Drug Dealers	Child Molesters
1) Food Stamps	Denied	**APPROVED**
2) Public Assistance	Denied	**APPROVED**
3) Public Housing	Denied	**APPROVED**
4) Financial Aid	Denied	**APPROVED**[33]

This shows that the government will assist those who forcibly molest children, who according to statistics, are primarily white males, but will hinder someone who sold drugs to a willing buyer, who is most likely a minority, who purchased it to either cope with stress, or for their own enjoyment.

This is why institutional racism is so dangerous. It attacks one group and assists another, while the scheme is knitted so intricately within formal policies and procedures until it is unseen by the victim. This puts the target of racism in a psychological state of confusion of not knowing why his circumstances are so dismal; while others who do more heinous crimes are much more fortunate.

AFRICAN AMERICAN SUCCESS...AND ITS CONSEQUENCES

Although for the most part, African American communities can be defined as ghettos, many people ask "what if things were different?" What if there was a revolutionary movement that produced professionals, a strong economic agenda, and other entities that would improve living conditions for African Americans?

There should be an optimistic approach when discussing how to overcome any social injustice; however, if we look throughout history, we will see that communal African American success is met with legislative obstacles, and, if that has little or no effect, met with violence by the city, state, and federal government. Greenwood, a district in Tulsa, Oklahoma was once one of the most successful and wealthiest African American communities in the United States during the early 20th Century; it was known as America's "Black Wall Street." The Tulsa Race Riot of 1921 was the death of that era. The riot was one of the most catastrophic race riots in history which completely leveled and destroyed Greenwood.

Oklahoma flourished during that time due to the oil boom. African Americans primarily lived in the Greenwood section. Because of segregation, African Americans were forced to patron their own businesses. The dollar would circulate Greenwood several times before leaving the community which fueled the African American owned businesses. The buildings on Greenwood Avenue facilitated the offices of almost all of Tulsa's black lawyers, realtors, doctors, and other professionals.[34]

On May 31, 2001 a race riot broke out after African Americans armed themselves in a pursuit to prevent a Greenwood man from being unjustifiably lynched for being falsely accused of trying to rape a white girl.

Riots ensued after the African Americans met with the whites from a lynch mob; the town was completely destroyed by white mobs and was the first U.S. city to ever have bombs dropped on it by law enforcement officials.[35] Over 600 successful businesses were destroyed. Among these were 30 grocery stores and two movie theaters, plus a hospital, a bank, a post office, libraries, 21 churches, 21 restaurants, schools, law offices, a half-dozen private airplanes and even a bus system. There was a total of $1.5 million in property damage (1921), which was an extremely large amount of money for that time.[36] June 29, 1921. Although the official death toll claimed by the authorities were that 26 blacks and 13 whites died during the riots, most estimates are considerably higher. The American Red Cross listed 8,624 persons in need of assistance, in excess of 1,000 homes and businesses destroyed, and the delivery of several stillborn infants.[37]

NEW YORK, NEW YORK BIG CITY OF DREAMS

Harlem, New York was given the nickname "Mecca" because it was the center of black culture going all the way back to the Harlem renaissance of the early nineteen hundreds. Many black authors, singers, dancers, and activists migrated to that area from different countries and regions of the United States. Harlem was the base for bigger national and international movements of almost anything relevant to African American culture, often referred to as the "Promised Land." However, New York is a good example of how back lash follows African American success in America.

During slavery, blacks were not victims of violence in New York until approaching the abolishment of slavery in 1863, during the New York draft riots. That was the first documented time that the black population in New York decreased, which was sparked after a forward progression of their social status. The second was in the 1990s, after African Americans excelled in their social status.

Despite that, African American New Yorkers became business owners, and got involved in politics for more than a century afterwards. The 1980s marked the most flamboyant, expressive era in African American history, where they wore expensive jewelry, drove fancy cars, and flaunted wealth that was extravagant for even white standards. New York City was the Mecca for this renaissance. Even the radio stations played songs like "Ain't No Stopping Us Now" which was an anthem for African American progress. New York City birthed Hip Hop in this decade; it was a style of music that, itself, was based off of boasting and showing success. The African American population increased in New York in this era and became so strong until they had their first African American Mayor in 1988, David Dinkins.

David Dinkins was known for his "nice guy" image.[38] He came in as a mayor that wanted to heal the bad race relations between the different ethnic groups in New York. He was sympathetic towards the needs of white New Yorkers which was reflected in his 1991 decision to make it illegal for companies within New York City to have business transactions with any companies in Ireland that discriminated against Catholics. He also increased the police department by 25%. Crime declined in the city the last 36 months of his 4 year term.[38] It was the first *decline* in crime in 30 years that that was increasing until his term which continuously decreased from 1990 until 5 mayoral terms after his.[39] To the surprise of many, it was him and not his predecessor, Rudolf Giuliani, that cleaned up the drug trafficking and prostitution around Times Square and revitalized it, and also persuading the Walt Disney Corporation to rehabilitate a dilapidated, but famous theater on 42nd Street. He also made it a duty to meet with the Jewish, Italian, and Hispanic communities as well. He had a major commitment to rehabilitating dilapidated housing in northern Harlem, the South Bronx and Brooklyn, despite significant budget constraints—he had more housing rehabilitated in a single term than Mr. Giuliani did in two terms; the USTA lease, which in its final form Mayor Bloomberg called "the only good athletic sports stadium deal, not just in New York but in the country"; and mental-health facility initiatives.[40] Despite all of his achievements, the biggest city in America having a Black mayor was a symbol of African American advancement and too much to stomach for many New Yorkers.

On August 19, 1991 at about 8:20 p.m., a 22 year old Jewish man, Yosef Lifsh, was heading west on President Street in a station wagon with three passengers acting as the last of a three-car motorcade of Rabbi Menachem Mendel Schneerson. At the intersection of President and Utica he ran a red light to catch up with the motorcade and struck a car going down Utica. He ended up on the sidewalk, knocking down a 600 pound stone pillar that fell on two children, Gavin Cato, 7, and his cousin, Angela Cato, 7. Gavin was killed and Angela was critically injured.

What infuriated the Caribbean and African American residents was that Lifsh was taken from the scene just a few minutes after the accident by a volunteer ambulance from the Hatzolah Ambulance Corps, while the black children lay under the stone pillar and were not removed by city ambulances workers for about ten minutes afterwards.[41]

There were already tensions between the African American and Jewish communities prior to the incident. The incident resulted in three days of rioting and looting and the murder of a Jewish man named Yankel Rosenbaum. Dinkins was reluctant to deploy vast numbers of police to crush the rioting because he had been elected as a peacemaker. However, his decision to use diplomacy instead of force resulted in the escalation of rioting where many Jewish New Yorkers criticized him for this. The first night of the riot, Dinkins and Police Commissioner Lee Brown, who was also an African American, went to Crown Heights to dismiss the false rumors about the circumstances surrounding the accident, such as the driver being intoxicated and preferential treatment given to the Jewish man by the Jewish ambulance corps; however, they had no impact on the rioters.[42]

In a speech on the Thanksgiving holiday following the riot, Dinkins denied that he had prevented police from protecting citizens in Crown Heights.[43] Many Jews expressed that Dinkins failed to contain the riot which was his responsibility as a mayor, to the detriment of the Jewish community.[44] The Crown Heights riot was an important issue raised repeatedly on the campaign trail. Rudolph Giuliani, who would become the next mayor of New York, called the Crown Heights riot a "pogrom" (an organized massacre against Jews) because "for three days people were beaten up because they were Jewish. "There's no question that not enough was done about it by the city of New York," stated one Jewish man prominent in political affairs.[45]

This exaggeration of the event led to the election of Rudolf Giuliani who himself led a "pogrom" against New Yorkers of African descent by using the NYPD. Giuliani started a street crimes unit that acted as a Gestapo squad in minority neighborhoods, which shook down and frisked as many as forty thousand African American, innocent law abiding citizens between 1996 and 1997 alone as an attempt to reduce crime.[46]

On February 4, 1999 four police officers from the street crimes unit shot to death an African immigrant, Amadou Diallo, in the vestibule of his building in the Bronx. Diallo, who was unarmed, "supposedly" matched the description of a serial rapist that police were looking for. In 1997 Abner Louimer, a Haitian immigrant, had his teeth knocked out and was then sodomized by the handle of a broom stick by a NYPD police officer in a precinct bathroom in Brooklyn after being arrested outside of a night club. During the ordeal the officer, Justin Volpe called Louima a nigger and said "It's Giuliani time."[47]

The officers involved in the Amadou Diallo case were not convicted of his murder and many other injustices meted out by the NYPD were left uncontested. The mayor's policies led to blatant discrimination against African Americans which trickled down to the rest of the city, affecting housing, employment, and the criminal justice system. Living conditions for African Americans became unbearable where it was, and still is, difficult to pay bills due to job discrimination and an open refusal to cooperate with them. The failure of the system to correct the system left many African Americans pessimistic about a future in New York City. Just between 2000 and 2004 the African American population decreased by 30,000.[48]

This was the first time that the African American population decreased in New York since the draft riots of the 1800's. As a consequence, valuable real estate, educational and job opportunities have been lost. This emigration destroyed communities throughout the city where there is no longer a strong sense of community due to the fact that neighborhoods are now filled with people that are strangers to one another, and communal ties have been cut that have existed for close to a century.

CONCLUSION

Institutional racism makes overcoming discrimination much more difficult because it is difficult to recognize the injustice and even more difficult to correct the problem because no clear culprit exists due to policies that "appear" to be applicable for everyone and made by the "system" instead of just one individual. Furthermore, an atmosphere is created that gives institutions, business, and the general public a negative attitude towards trusting, respecting, and recognizing the potential that minorities have in making positive contributions, whether it's in employment or the society in general. It reaches the extent where it becomes an unspoken boycott that affects the way everything is done, from traffic stops to job interviews to housing policies (just to name a few).

The reader should understand that discussing this problem is an integral part of Islam, because the Prophet Muhammad himself was oppressed, and the Quran is against oppression and racism. Making hijrah from Mecca to Medina was the solution that Allah (س) prescribed for him. The Quran prescribes many solutions for overcoming social inequalities that are simple and effective. The second half of this book not only offers the solutions, but lays out in detail the applications where anyone can take advantage of it; however, be aware that backlash follows minority success.

Furthermore, the main point being made is that things such as the federal sentencing laws are just one of many ways the Judeo-Christian West have obstructed the success of the so-called descendants of Ham. Through two decades of discriminatorily longer prison sentences, African American males are now more abundant in the penile system than in higher education. The government knew what the effects would be by passing these laws. However, "have African Americans ever existed in the United States without being targeted to be placed in captivity and performing free labor?"

In the case of the Crown Heights riots, the death of one Jewish man led to the justification of Dinkins' successor, Giuliani, to form a Gestapo unit that harassed, shot, brutalized peoples of color, and arrested tens of thousands of law abiding African American and Latino New Yorkers for more than a decade afterwards. This was a result of a "squeamishness" that came from any open display of power by minorities.

The reader should not dismiss this issue as being just a speculative analysis of a law that just coincidentally affects one group. I challenge the reader to randomly visit any major U.S. city and assess the living conditions of the African American communities.

For some, these realities are nothing new. For them, the answer to the problem is much more important than the obvious circumstances. Therefore, the solution to not being a victim of institutional racism is to avoid falling into the negative stereotypes and never become too comfortable with yourself where you forget the stealth nature of institutional racism.

In some instances, people are falsely accused of crimes, or targeted by the "system." In other cases, the dilemma of chasing the "glitter" is the dilemma. High ethical standards and self dependency are mandatory to avoid this trap; they are easier to live up to for those who are taught them from the beginning of their childhoods until adulthood is reached. The powerful are fully aware of this; therefore, the easiest way for them to create social discord and maintain their status is through creating a disorganized family structure. The following chapter is designed to help the reader understand the societal elements that are responsible for defragmenting that institution.

CHAPTER 4

The Destruction of Family

America leads the world in divorce rates and single parent families, and, at the same time, leads the world in the highest prison populations. There is a definite connection between the two. Since this book is about oppression, I must deal with the causes of crime simply because incarceration is probably *the* most oppressive situation imaginable: not being able to see one's family, being woke up by shouting whistle blowing officers for strip searches, being released with no rights, and having very few means of making a legitimate living after release because of a felony conviction on a job application, etc.

Prior to sentencing, judges order a presentence investigation of the defendant's life in order to see what caused that person to do what he or she did. A bad child hood is what is known as "mitigating" circumstances. This gives the judge the ability to lessen the sentence since the child was "nurtured" to do what he did more than "chose" to deviate from a good way of life provided by parents.

An organization based in Washington, D.C. called *The Institute for Marriage and Public Policy* did a study in 2005 based on 23 different U.S. studies that examined the effects of family life on crime. Of the 23 studies reviewed, all but three found that family structure had an effect on crime or delinquency. In 19 of these 23 studies where a family structure effect was found, children from non-intact or single parent families had higher rates of crime or delinquency. The overall study demonstrated that married parents reduced both the individual risk and the overall rates of crime. It also showed a higher probability for teens that lived in a single parent home to break the law. Also, areas with high rates of family fragmentation have higher crime rates as a result.[1]

AN ECONOMIC NEED

Just as slavery, robbery, and almost all other injustices are economically inspired, so was the scheme of familial division. Today, dysfunctional families are a reality for many Americans despite race; however, it was first forced on African Americans shortly after the discovery of America. The idea was created to meet an economic need of slave owners. Usually the men and women slaves were separated to prevent a sense of community and pride from developing which would lead to slave revolts. Secondly, slavery could only be an effective institution if the will, dignity, and pride of the strongest were destroyed. The *image* of the strongest would also have to be destroyed to instill in everyone fear on the premise that "if master could do this to the strongest, imagine what he could do to the average?"

Although the concept started out as a tactic to control slaves during the colonial period, it has spread far beyond race, where "all" ethnic groups have become affected by it. The originator of this idea was a slave owner, Willie Lynch. His guide, *Let's Make a Slave*, was written for slave owners that had difficulty controlling their slaves. His advice was that the toughest meanest slave should be beaten to almost death in front of the others, especially his woman, and made an example that only the plantation master was powerful. The male was less than a woman, creating the following results.

(Caution! The following excerpts may be offensive.)

Let us make a slave. What do we Need?....
THE BREAKING PROCESS OF THE AFRICAN WOMAN....
Therefore, we shall go deeper into this area of the subject matter concerning what we have produced here in this breaking of the female

nigger. We have reversed the relationship. In her natural uncivilized state she would have a strong dependency on the uncivilized nigger male, and she would have a limited protective dependency toward her independent male offspring and would raise female offspring to be dependent like her. Nature had provided for this type of balance. We reversed nature by burning a dependent like her. Nature had provided for this type of balance. We reversed nature by burning and pulling one civilized nigger apart and bull whipping the other to the point of death--all in her presence. By her being left alone, unprotected, with the male image destroyed, the ordeal caused her to move from her psychological dependent state to a frozen independent state. In this frozen psychological state of independence she will raise her male and female offspring in reversed roles. For fear of the young male's life she will psychologically train him to be mentally weak and dependent, but physically strong. Because she has become psychologically independent, she will train her female offspring to be psychological independent as well. What have you got? You've got the nigger woman out front and the nigger man behind and scared. This is perfect situation for sound sleep and economics. Before the breaking process, we had to be alert and on guard at all times. Now we can sleep soundly, for out of frozen fear, his woman stand guard for us. He cannot get past her early infant slave molding process. He is a good tool, now ready to be tied to the horse at a tender age. By the time a nigger boy reaches the age of sixteen, he is soundly broken in and ready for a long life of sound and efficient work and the reproduction of a unit of good labor force...

(By The Black Arcade Liberation Library; 1970 [recompiled and reedited by Kenneth T. Spann])

Some people may feel that this was a long time ago and no longer exists. Although the bull whip is obsolete, the technique is still applied, mainly through the criminal justice system. Male professional athletes may appear powerful while tackling and slam dunking on television; however, they are usually slammed in court by judges during divorces and child custody cases. These court proceedings are negative on the family structure because they put two family members against one another, leaving one as a victor and the other as a loser, where the child ends up taking sides with one over the other.

Although money is essential to the children's development, court ordered child support was not created for the benefit of the children. It was formed by the state to prevent people from relying on the system for public assistance and being a strain on public funds. In many instances it is required only after a parent asks for some government support: food stamps, subsidized housing, etc. The child support stops at money. The courts do not require any type of spiritual, mental, psychological, emotional, or moral support from the fathers. In turn, this allows the child to simply have the food and clothing provisions to grow strong, but to be morally, spiritually, mentally, and psychologically weak. The children will then grow up as just a clump of meat to join the work force in the same light that Willie Lynch predicted centuries ago: a weak dependent male.

Outside of domestic issues, the justice system is "anti-male" in general. Justice Department statics show that when a man and a woman are convicted of the same crime, the tougher sentence is imposed on the man. A man convicted of murder is about twenty times more likely to receive the death penalty than a woman, despite that the circumstances of the crime are identical. [8]

Entertainment

The entertainment world is just as dangerous because it subliminally feeds the public the image of the weak purposeless male, until that attitude is wide spread and deep rooted. Shows like *Martin*, *The Dave Chappelle Show*, *Everybody Hates Chris*, and even the Tyler Perry series of films show males that are physically big and strong, but are man handled and intimidated by their women. They also attempt to portray the uselessness of the male. Because these types of shows are comedies they make it not just acceptable, but enjoyable for both men and women to live out these roles.

Feeling that the male has virtually no power verses a woman leaves many women with the belief that a man's power is reduced to his financial contributions, and not his ability to provide any form of guidance or leadership. This also leads to the self defeating attitude that many fathers have which dissuades them from contributing to their children's development. Many that I have spoken to expressed that they have lost concern as trying to be involved on the basis that their presence is not important because the mother's resistance will be supported by an "anti-male" judicial system that will support her claims whether they are true or false. Most are so "psychologically" defeated until they will not even try to exhaust all legal options to resolve their problems, even in instances where it is obvious that the system will favor them over their children's mother.

RELIGION AND FAMILY

Male leadership of the family is just as much a Biblical belief as it is Islamic. As stated in the opening chapter, the Quran was sent to confirm the truths that came before it. Both the Bible and the Quran place an emphasis on the importance of family and its structure. Just as a bank or any other institution is set up with certain individuals to carry out specific duties, the Bible and the Quran assign the duty of leadership to the husband. The Bible reads:

> 22. Wives, submit yourselves unto your own husbands, as unto the Lord.
> 23. For the husband is the head of the wife, even as Christ is the head of the church: and he is the Savior of the body.
> 24. Therefore as the church is subject unto Christ, so let the wives be to their own husbands in everything. (Ephesians 5:22-24)
> 11. But I would have you know, that the head of every man is Christ; and the head of the woman is the man; and the head of Christ is God. (Corinthians 11:3)

The Quran reads, "Men have authority over women on account of the qualities with which God hath caused the one of them to excel the other and for what they (men are required to) spend of their prosperity." (Quran 2:36)

Not only should we look at the scriptures as a source of guidance, but investigate and verify that the application of these solutions is sound. The best way is to analyze countries that have a more "theological" based government, where male leadership is dominant in family life

THE ISLAMIC WORLD'S COHESIVE FAMILY STRUCTURE AND THEIR LOW CRIME RATE

In order for us to grow, we must separate ourselves from previous beliefs and honestly ask ourselves questions that may benefit us without letting our emotional connection to what is dear to us from accepting the truth. It's similar to the person that ignores their spouse's lie of being faithful and discredits the evidences from voice mail, letters, eyewitness accounts, and numerous other sources that prove infidelity, simply because there is too much pain involved in accepting the truth.

It may be hard to swallow, however, besides Iraq, Afghanistan, and other regions of the Islamic World that have been occupied by foreign armies, the Muslim world has far less crime and social problems than Western nations. Although people are caught up into the façade that the United States is a civilized society with higher moral standards than the Islamic world, statistics show differently. Just the murder rate alone is lower in countries that American politicians accuse of being world threats and forces that must be stopped. Most recent statistics cite the United States as having a 5.4 percent murder rate per every 100,000 people verses Iran at 2.93, Syria at 1.14, and Lebanon at only .57.[9]

At the same time, the United States and other non-Islamic nations, lead the world with their high crime rates.[10]

Countries with the highest reported crime rate

Countries	Total Crimes
United States	11,877,218
United Kingdom	6,523,706
Germany	6,507,394
France	3,771,850
Russia	2,952,370
Japan	2,853,739
South Africa	2,683,849
Canada	2,516,918
Italy	2,231,550
India	1,764,630[11]

The two biggest theories behind the Islamic world as having a low crime rate is because of its relatively low level of development, which has a positive effect on crime rates, and that the strictness of Islamic penal law deters many from breaking it. This first theory is not sound in the least because highly developed nations in the Islamic world still have lower homicide rates than the United States (5.4): Saudi Arabia (.92), Qatar (.77), Bahrain (.95), Kuwait (.99).[12] Secondly, states such as Virginia, Florida, and Texas that have capital punishment still have higher murder and crime rates than Islamic nations. This brings us to a third theory, and perhaps the most sound, which is that Islam places more emphasis on family structure and the importance of male leadership, which adds confidence, emotional stability, and guidance to their children's lives. Divorce is considered the most displeasing thing to the creator that is permissible. When it is permitted, the children are preferably placed in the custody of the father. Divorce rates are lower in the Islamic world, so usually there are both parents in the home.

More responsibility is placed on the father who will most likely add a firmer structure to the children's rearing. Although men are given the position of authority, they also have the responsibility of being providers in Islam. Despite western misconceptions, the women are freer than the men in terms of familial responsibilities.

THE NEED FOR A FATHER

With the growth of the pharmaceutical industry comes an increase in the amount of children being prescribed prescription drugs. The newest and most common "disorder" for boys is ADD. Instead of physicians prescribing exercise and other constructive activities to help boys channel their energy, they prescribe medication. Many single mothers don't dispute the doctors' decisions simply because they don't understand that it is unnatural for a boy to sit still with his hands folded all day without asking questions or exerting himself physically. In many instances the only problem that these boys have is being boys. The bigger problem is that they are developing drug dependencies at an early age and told repeatedly that something is wrong with them. Both will have long term negative effects that they will carry with them into their adult lives.

I can see their future in the lives of so many of my child hood friends that grew up under identical circumstances that are now in prison, or virtually destroyed from drugs or alcohol abuse. It reminded me of the consequences that many males have of being deprived of a male role model that can offer life experiences, guidance, and structure.

As my childhood friend, Jeffrey Rodriguez, who spent half his life in trouble with the law stated in a letter that he recently wrote to me from prison: "Always keep in mind before you react that you have a little man who needs you in his life, and he's at that age where all he was taught when it comes to morals and values apply, or the streets get the best of him; and we both know what it is to be raised without the guidance of a father… dig me…"[13]

In his situation, Jeffrey's father was killed in the Bronx during a robbery by heroin addicts when he was a child. My friend spent half of his life in and out of prison, doing things that he believed were normal for a man to do.

Mike Tyson was raised in Brownsville, Brooklyn by his mother, getting in trouble as a young teenager without any authoritative male figure in his life. He stayed in trouble with the law until he went to a reformatory and met his mentor and father figure Cuss D'Amato. With his guidance, Tyson became heavy weight champion of the world at the age of 19. Once D'Amato died, Tyson fell right back into the same negative patterns as he did as a child. Later on he found himself in trouble with the law again. As Tyson explains:

> I lost that belief in myself once Cuss died. When I was a kid I used to love to hear that ole 'refuse to lose' and all these great quotes and poems. I lost that when I lost my mentor, I lost my friend, all that stuff died when he died.
>
> It stems from my childhood. I never had the tools that a basic child had: the mother, the father, and the whole traditional family, where we work out problems, I never lived that particular type of life. I always looked out for me, me, me, and if there's a problem I'm going to handle it my way, or else I'm going to run. I was never able to cipher a problem

out, decode a problem, everything was totally cryptic to me. When it got too cryptic I booted it out the situation.[14]

Many of the unfortunate may say, "I'm a product of my environment." However, even within the darkest ghettos we can find success stories of those that overcame negative influences and obstacles in their environment. Collin Powell grew up in the South Bronx, which from my knowledge and experience of living there, has always been a high crime area. In his book "My American Journey" he describes his father as being the "warden." He was very stern, and instilled in Collin Powell a fear of submitting to the vices of the neighborhood. With this authoritative figure over his shoulder, Powell became a general and the third most powerful man in the Bush administration: Secretary of State.

There are a lot of other potential leaders and powerful peoples whose talents are rarely harnessed into molding them into positions consistent with their natural capabilities due to the lack of these same types of authoritative male role models.

For these reasons Islam places the responsibility of "raising" the child on the shoulders of the father. Donald Trump, who is often praised for his business wit, accredits his success to his father's personally habits that followed closely as a child:

> It's great to have good natural instincts, but even if you do, you may find that's not enough. Over the years I've come up with certain rules for myself that are important—and in some cases vital—for surviving the perils of success.
> The first and most important of these is **be disciplined.**
> Discipline is something I learned from watching my father, Fred Trump—the kind of man who stays the course during good times and bad. It's the key to staying on top. It means you go to work each morning (as my father still does), and you consistently do the things that you know will get results. You push forward, then you push forward some more, and you never let your adversaries see you worried...[15]

CONCLUSION

This chapter didn't address the never ending debate between Islam and the Western world on which one brings more contentment to women's lives. That would be a separate book by itself, which boils down to a matter of opinion of whether a cloth is considered oppressive if it's placed on a woman's head verses around her shoulders or waist (western culture). The nature of the Quran's message to family structure is identical to the Bible's; therefore, there is no difference in that regards. This means that western family structures, for the most part, are actually a deviation from the ideology that it claims to be attached to.

Secondly, we shouldn't be influenced by the language of the media that constantly uses the word "freedom" to describe western relationship with women. Women being twice as likely to be victims of violent crimes in the United States is evidence that Western culture and laws do not protect women. However, the word "freedom" is tossed around to play a psychological game to make people believe that showing more of their body than the Islamic world does, or going wherever they want from night until dusk is enjoyment. Freedom is a word that just the mere idea of having it is pleasure within itself without even taking the time to analyze what is freedom, and, outside of the media's version, do people really feel free in the West? Freedom in the western media translates into being wild and not having to follow rules even if they're beneficial. It means that one is free to destroy his or her own self; whereas, freedom in the Islamic world means to be free from things that are destructive. It means that freedom is a state of being that comes from one knowing that he or she is safe from oppressive elements such as crime, drug dependency, incarceration, emotionally instability, disease, spiritual weakness, and poverty.

These are all oppressive circumstances that we see in western societies which "appear" as though they are the results of individual decisions; however, they are merely "symptoms" of a bigger problem. The dilemma is that Western societies have implemented the "Willie Lynch" teachings and created a system that reverses the roles between men and women through entertainment, media outlets, and the judicial system. Family is commonly viewed as being more of a burden than a benefit, while the character and image of men has been portrayed as weak and useless. It has trickled down to the masses where male credibility, purpose, and authority have been destroyed to keep society disorganized and weak.

With a chaotic, disorganized society you have more people in prison, on drugs and alcohol, and struggling to overcome their personal dilemmas due to being groomed into adults with very little structure and direction.

Therefore, the Quran's purpose is to free mankind from these oppressive circumstances through making sure men utilize their innate talent of leadership while acting as providers: "Men have authority over women on account of the qualities with which God hath caused the one of them to excel the other and for what they (men are required to) spend of their prosperity." (Quran 2:36). In the case of Muslims, it is incumbent on men to *take* authoritative positions in the home, even if you have to continuously struggle to do so through dialogue, reason, and as a last resort, the judicial system.

Although western media outlets have skillfully influenced the masses into believing they are free, when we look at how many run on the nonstop economic tread mill, serving others to maintain what they have, we see that most of their time is consumed to maintain "freedom" in the service of someone else. Therefore, the destruction of family is a root that leads to many branches of oppression, the most harmful being economic.

CHAPTER 5

Usury, and the Bait to Success

USURY

We live in a society whose forms of oppression are as advanced as the time that we live in. Like the Bible, the Quran recognizes usury as being a form of oppression; however, the Quran sternly warns the Muslims not to practice usury in their business affairs:

275. Those who swallow interest will not (be able to) stand (in resurrection) except as standeth one who Satan hath confounded with his touch; this is because they say, trade is only like (earning) interest, whereas God hath decreed trade lawful and hath forbidden interest, wherefore whosoever (after) the admonition hath come unto him from his Lord desists, shall have what hath gone before; and his affair rests with God, and whoever returneth (to it even after the admonition); They are the inmates of the (Hell) fire, therein shall they abide.
276. God blotteth out (the gains of) interest and causeth charities to grow; God loveth not any ingrate sinner...
280. And if (any debtor) be in straightened circumstances, then let there be respite until (he is in) ease; and that if ye forego it (even the capital) (as charity) it is better for you if ye only knew. (Quran 2:275-76, 280)

Free trade, loans, and investments are permissible in Islam; usury and charging debtors extraordinarily high late fees is not. Loans are permissible in Islam as long as there is no interest attached to them. Due to the depreciation of paper currency, interest is only permitted at a low rate to keep up with the rate of inflation, which is usually an amount so small that the lender does not make a profit. Interest is considered to be a tactic to keep the borrower in a subservient economic position, which is why Islam forbids the Muslims from practicing it.

If a loan is used to pursue a business venture, the borrower may, or may not be successful in establishing what he or she intended to accomplish. The same holds true in other situations such as student loans, where the education obtained may not provide the borrower with adequate employment to pay the loan back as promptly as expected.

Therefore, Islam permits the borrower and lender to form an agreement that allows the borrower to share a percentage of the profits that have been earned through that particular business venture. This can be paid to the lender in addition to the initial amount borrowed. Collateral should also be established to make sure that the lender does not suffer a loss if the loan is not paid back. The sum of money paid back to the lender may vary, depending upon the amount made in profits, as well as the actual percentage agreed to by the two parties.

This is known in Arabic as an *ishtiraak*, which means a *partnership*. It does not permit one party to exploit the other. Although one party may be in a more favorable economic position, fairness and equality is administered throughout the entire process.

THE TRAGEDY OF INTEREST

We live in a capitalistic society where an extravagant, fictitious way of living is marketed as a *must* when it comes to obtaining happiness. The only way that "most" people can live the status quo "six-figure-salary" way of life is outside of the law, or through *borrowing money*.

Loans and credit cards are the common solutions, but have high interest rates and outrageously high penalty fees for late payments. The borrower is usually placed in a situation where just paying the interest is often the main objective. The amount paid in the end is often much higher than the amount borrowed. Actually, credit cards, student loans, car loans, and home mortgages are liabilities that often exceed the assets of those who were influenced to believe that they would be their stepping-stone to success.

The average person that borrows money is usually poor and doesn't understand how compound interest works. They don't realize that a loan they thought would be paid off in five years may take ten years or even longer to repay. There is usually a high level of frustration in paying it back.

Tragedies such as the holocaust were actually fueled off of usury which Adolf Hitler referred to as "slave interest" in his autobiography *Mein Kampf*.[1] Although Hitler and the Nazis were racists, and their actions could not be justified, much of the German animosity towards the Jews during the earlier twentieth century was based on the fact that Jews controlled the banking institutions. Germany's debt was so deep until their currency was worthless. Adolf Hitler was deeply inspired to push his campaign of the breaking of usury after listening to a speech by an economist named Gottfried Feder:

> When listening to Gottfried Feder's first lecture about the 'Breaking of the Tyranny of Interest,' I knew immediately that the question involved was a theoretical truth which would reach enormous importance for the German people's future. The sharp separation of the stock exchange capital from the national economy offered the possibility of fighting the internationalization of German economic life, without threatening with the fight against capital in general, also the basis of an independent folk autonomy. Germany's development already stood before my eyes too clearly for me not to know that the hardest battle had to be fought, not against hostile nations, but rather against international capital. In Feder's lecture I sensed a powerful slogan for this coming fight.[2]

HOW IS INTEREST TYRANNICAL?

The only way new currency (which is not actual money, but credit representing a debt), enters circulation is through it being borrowed from bankers. When the State and population borrow large sums, we "appear" to succeed. In actuality, the bankers only make the amount of the principal of every loan, never the additional sum required to pay the interest. The new money never equals the new debt. The amounts needed to pay the interest on loans do not exist because it was never created.

Under these circumstances, where new debt is greater than new money, the total debt steadily outstrips the amount of currency that exists to pay the debt. The people can never, under any circumstance, get out of debt.

Take the following example to understand the "tyranny of interest", as explained by Darren Perkins:

> When someone goes borrows $100,000 to purchase a home, the bank clerk has the borrower agree to pay back the loan plus interest. At 8.25% interest for 30 years, the borrower must agree to pay $751.27 per month for a total of $270,456.00.
>
> The clerk then requires the citizen to assign to the banker the right of ownership of the property if the borrower does not make the required payments. The bank clerk then gives the borrower a $100,000 check or a $100,000 deposit slip, crediting the borrower's checking account with $100,000.
>
> The borrower then writes checks to the builder, subcontractors, etc. who in turn write checks. $100,000 of new "checkbook" money is thereby added to the "money in circulation."
>
> However, this is the fatal flaw in the system: the only new money created and put into circulation is the amount of the loan, $100,000. The money to pay the interest is NOT created, and therefore was NOT added to "money in circulation."
>
> Even so, this borrower (and those who follow him in ownership of the property) must earn and take out of circulation $270,456.00, $170,456.00 more than he put in circulation when he borrowed the original $100,000! (This interest cheats all families out of nicer homes. It is not that they cannot afford them; it is because the bankers' interest forces them to pay for nearly 3 homes to get one!)
>
> Every new loan puts the same process in operation. Each borrower adds a small sum to the total money supply when he borrows, but the

payments on the loan (because of interest) then deduct a much larger sum from the total money supply.

There is therefore no way all debtors can pay off the money lenders. As they pay the principle and interest, the money in circulation disappears. All they can do is struggle against each other, borrowing more and more from the money lenders each generation. The money lenders (bankers), who produce nothing of value, gradually gain a death grip on the land, buildings, and present and future earnings of the whole working population....[3]

Not only have people as individuals fell into this trap, but even entire communities and nations, as described by Professor Randall Robinson in *The Debt*:

...Since the mid-1980s African countries have transferred three billion dollars out of Africa to the IMF alone. Overall, these countries spend four times more on debt service to Western creditors than they do on health care and education for their citizens. They are even pressured by the IMF to grow export crops in order to earn the hard currency necessary to service Western debt that never grows smaller. Sub-Saharan Africa's overwhelming debt totals more than 230 billion dollars, with thirty three of its forty-four countries as heavily indebted poor countries by the World Bank...[4]

THE OBVIOUS

It is the Bible, not the Quran, that advocates interest as a tactic to the Israelites to keep people subservient: "For the Lord thy God blesseth thee, as he promised thee: and thou shalt lend to many, but thou shalt not borrow; and they shalt not reign over thee" (Deuteronomy 15: 6). Notice how the Israelites (Jews) are commanded to lend to many nations but borrow from none. If the Israelites are to be leaders of the world, it would be impossible for them to be in debt to the people they are to rule. The lender always has the upper hand. The borrower is always in a vulnerable and subservient position and actually a servant of the interest attached to the loan. The rewards of lending have been made clear, where the Bible states, "...and thou shalt reign over many nations, but they shall not reign over thee."

Although the Zionist controlled media portrays Jews as being victims, this shows that Judaism is a religion based off of economic exploitation, where they can keep those in a subservient economic position who are not of the bloodline of Isaac, but everyone else is fair game.

In the documentary *The Obama Deception* by Alex Jones, the ruling elite, bankers, and other institutions are fingered as looters who have hijacked the United States economy: Bilderburg Group, Chatham house council on Foreign Relations, members of the *Trilateral Commission,* and Council on Foreign Relations (CFR), Timothy Geithner Secretary of Treasury, Robert Rueben, Rueben Sommers, Allen Greenspan, Henry Kissinger, Richard Hass, and **Robert Zoelick**, President of the World Bank. However, no emphasis is placed on the fact that all of these individuals are Jews and groups ran by Zionists.

This is not written to plant a seed of hatred against Jews, but to enlighten the reader on the fact that their economic situation is influenced by a religiously justified economic oppression. Keep in mind that there is a much higher percentage of Jews that control the monetary system than are represented in the national population. New York City having the largest Jewish population in the world outside of Israel and having the most influential stock market in the world (Wall Street) is not a coincidence. Many would say that I as an author would not object to this if it were Muslims who were in power. In power, no, but in power through economic trickery that leaves the common man believing that getting himself into debt is his key to success, yes. Furthermore, just realizing that you are in the midst of an economic "jihad" is the beginning of overcoming it.

I challenge the reader to also do an independent study to test these premises. The west paints the façade that they are not "anti-Semitic"; however, it was England that expelled the Jews from it (1290 A.D. to 1656), known as the *Edict of Expulsion* by Edward I, because they manipulated the English economy with an extortionate form of usury.

THE BAIT TO SUCCESS

They ask thee concerning wine (strong drink) and gambling.
Say: "In them is great sin and some profit for men;
but the sin is greater than the profit."
They ask thee how much they are to spend (in Charity);
say: "What is beyond your needs."
Thus doth Allah make clear to you His Signs: in order that ye may consider. (Qur'an 2:219)

Other than loans, casinos and internet cafes that offer gambling are the new traps that offer fantasy like quick fixes to long term dilemmas. They can be found all throughout the United States. The Casinos are abundant in cities in the rust belt, in minority communities, Native American reservations, and other economically depressed regions with high unemployment. They are welcomed with open arms to provide jobs that will replace the ones lost from the car, steel, and other industries; however, according to an extensive report done by Earl L. Grinols (Uni-versity of Illinois) and David B. Mustard (University of Georgia) the existence of a casino means a long term increase in the crime rate (robbery, homicide, prostitution, theft, burglary, and drug related offenses).[5]

Moreover, these institutions are generally placed directly in minority communities as explained by William N. Thompson in *Gambling: an encyclopedia of histories, issues, and society:*

> Minority people and persons of lower income who live together in poorer communities have often been targeted by banks and gambling entrepreneurs as being good potential players. Government lotteries have been faulted for directing marketing campaigns at minority communities with advertisements suggesting that gambling is "the way out" of the ghetto. Also, as states such as Illinois purposely located casino facilities in communities needing economic development, they caused casinos to be very near minority people. Such being the case, African Americans and others living close to the casinos had a much higher level of participation in gambling than did other people.[6]

Similarly to both gambling and interest are other modern schemes that Islam forbids because they exploit the hard work of those at the bottom while the leaders do nothing but count money. Amongst other trends are those that try to incorporate the masses of the poor within the pyramid of the larger organization with hopes of success such as the network marketing scams. Wealthy professionals have websites and brochures with pictures of them posing on an exotic beach with drinks in their hands, trying to portray the image that they made a fortune from selling a product such as an energy drink, weight loss powders, etc. More emphasis is put on getting new members to get others to sign in under them instead of the product, which is used as a cover up to disguise the pyramid.

This is no different from interest, because the person on top only sits back and collects money while others do the work. Secondly, I've learned from personal experience that the people that start these schemes made their wealth through studying hard in college and becoming professionals, or investing a lot of time working, and making wise investments.

CONCLUSION

Gambling and interest are made forbidden in the Quran because they lead to oppressive circumstances. Pyramid schemes and any other form of capital gain that is based off of the exploitation of others are also forbidden.

Usury, criminalization, slavery, and sanctioning what roles people must fulfill in society are all tactics used to oppress. The Quran is opposed to getting into debt and being exploited by usury to attempt to reverse one's economic situation. This information was not brought forth to create hatred, but to illustrate the consequences of resorting to loans or credit, or by getting in debt in general to attempt to reverse one's economic situation.

One may conclude that oppressive elements exist in all societies; however, the premise for doing so cannot be traced to any type of Quranic text. The nature of the Bible in relation to racism and oppression is distinctly different from the egalitarian nature of the Quran, as the reader shall see in the following chapters.

CHAPTER 6

The Quran Verses Islamic Society: separating the two

In order to understand the Quran's position in relation to racism and oppression, we must not only analyze Muslim's actions, but the Quran's text. Then, we must see if the Quran was either referred to as the justification of an oppressive or racist action, or was the action a deviation from the Quran.

To begin with, there is no such thing as a "chosen people" or "holy" bloodline in the Quran. Oppression and racism in the Muslim world has been a result of either foreign influence, or those who chose to deviate from Islam to pursue other objectives. Saddam Hussein led a Bathist government founded on "Arab nationalism" and not Islamic law, which actually mimicked western governments in its legislative structure. Some predominantly Muslim societies have even been influenced by tribal customs and forged *ahadith* that contradict all Quranic teachings.

Despite this, the Islamic world has remained triumphant in displaying how a theocratic society can transcend racial barriers as explained by J. Spencer Trimingham in *Africa a Handbook to the Continent*:

> Islam is a force which can, given the chance, revolutionize the life of Africans because it is a civilization. Its effect upon Africa, where it has had an undisputed field of propaganda for many centuries until

European powers extended their control during the eighties of the last century, is often ignored; all the stress being placed upon the more recent effect of Western civilization. But if we are to make a true estimate of what is happening in Africa, Islam, as a force which transcends racial and political barriers, is obviously a power to be reckoned with.[1]

Bernard Lewis, Emeritus Professor of Near East Studies at Princeton University, has written a multitude of works on this subject. In his book *Islam in History*, he states:

> It is often said that Islam is an egalitarian religion. There is much truth in this assertion. If we compare the principles and to a large extent even the practice of Islam at the time of its advent with the societies that surrounded it—the stratified feudalism of Iran, the caste system of India, the privileged aristocracies of both Byzantine and Latin Europe—the Islamic dispensation did indeed bring a message of equality. Not only did Islam not endorse such systems of social and tribal differentiation; it explicitly and resolutely rejected them. The Quran is quite specific. (49:13)[2]

Islam offers specific guidelines for economical, political, and social interactions through the Quran and traditions (*Sunnah*). The Quran states that Allah (س) has administered justice by creating the Universe with *balance*, known in the Arabic language as *mizan* (The Quran 42:17; 55:7-9; 57:25; 101:6-9). For this reason, Islam forbids all forms of oppression and inequality.

Considering that it is not always easy to do what is necessary to "establish" equality in society, it is referred to as the "steep path" in the Quran (90:12-14). The Quran requires Muslims to make sure that no one is abased below the other or neglects to provide the indigent with basic necessities while others hoard wealth:

> 12. What would make thee know what is the steep path?
> 13. (It is) the freeing a slave or a captive.
> 14. Or feeding in the day of hunger… (Quran 90:12-14)

ISLAM'S FIGHT AGAINST OPPRESSION

Islam does not permit the oppression or exploitation of any individual or group, including non-Muslims. The only occasion the Quran permits the Muslims to seize wealth, property, or land is when it is compensation for victims, where the Muslims are not the aggressors: "That (shall be so); and he who did retaliate with the like of that which he hath been wronged, and again he hath been aggressed, most certainly God will aid him; Verily God is the Most Merciful, Oft-Forgiving." (Quran 22:60).

Because Islam is a religion that is based on justice, it allows people to liberate themselves from oppression and establish equality. Once liberated, they are permitted to seek compensation for their sufferings:

"41. And whosoever defendeth himself (in avenging) after being oppressed, then against these there is no way (to blame). 42. The way (to blame) is against those who do injustice unto the people and transgress in the earth unjustly; these, for them shall be a painful chastisement." (Quran 42:41-42).

JIHAD

Fighting or struggling in the path of God is called *jihad* in Islam, which comes from the verb *"jahada"* (to strive). There are four basic types of jihad. The first type of jihad is known as *jihad bin-nafs*: the *struggle with one's own inner self*. This has often been considered the greatest jihad, or in Arabic *jihad al-akbar* (Quran 9:41). There is *jihad bil-maal*: to *spend one's wealth in the path of Islam* (Quran 9:41). The third form is *jihad bil-'ilm: fighting to obtain or spread knowledge*. Knowledge is obtained or spread to improve the conditions of society, without the desire to obtain any profit from the effort. The fourth is *jihad bis-saif: fighting by the sword*. This is resorted to when all other options have been exhausted to remedy an injustice, or in the course of defending the Muslims.

Physical aggression is only permissible as a last alternative to defend one's self or to seek justice for any wrong committed. In this type of circumstance, compensation may also be sought to demand that balance is meted out.

During the beginning of the Prophet Muhammad's (ص) mission, captives were taken along with the spoils of war by the Muslim soldiers. These captives were often forced to do labor as compensation to the Muslims for their suffering and hardships which were inflicted by the forces that the captives belonged to. It was only permitted to force people into servitude in times of war, where the Muslims were not the aggressors, but defenders of equality and justice. This was a result of the Muslims being forced out of Mecca and having their possessions stolen from them because they accepted one God instead of the many that the Pagan clans had.

THE QURAN'S ATTEMPT TO ABOLISH SLAVERY

The abolishment of alcohol in early Islamic times began with the commandment to "not come to prayer intoxicated"(4:43). It was "slightly" acceptable outside of prayer. It was then made completely forbidden (5:90-91). Most Arabs would not have given it up immediately, which would have made it an almost impossible rule to follow. Slavery was permitted with limitations because it, too, was to eventually be completely forbidden like alcohol. The Quran doesn't attack slavery, but places praise on setting slaves free which is equivalent to its abolition, that is, for those that want to do good.

However, it would be preposterous to believe that the slave traders of the Prophet Muhammad's (ص) time would magically be persuaded to lose their fortunes that the trade brought on the premise that "Allah (س) said it is bad". Therefore, wisdom had to be used in order to eliminate it gradually, as the Quran states:

> And call them unto the way of thy Lord with *wisdom* and kindly exhortation and dispute with them in the manner which is the best; verily the Lord knoweth better of him who hath gone astray from His path; and He knoweth best of those guideth aright. (Quran 16:125).

Although forced servitude was tolerated during the early Islamic period, the slave trade that existed amongst the polytheists during the life of the Prophet Muhammad (ص) was significantly reduced because the Quran placed great emphasis on how virtuous it was to free slaves. The freeing of a slave was considered to be an expiation of a sin. Freeing a slave, or in some circumstances, freeing numerous slaves was prescribed for those who violated certain Islamic commandments such as neglecting to fast during the month of Ramadan or the deliberate breaking o one's oath:

> 89. God doth not call you to account for what is vain in your oaths, but He calleth you to account for the making of deliberate oaths; so its expiation is the feeding of ten poor men out of the moderate food you feed your families with, or their clothing or the freeing of a slave... (Quran 5:89)

Another violation that constituted the freeing of a slave was when someone divorced their wife through what was known as *zihaar*. During pre-Islamic and early Islamic times, Arab men would often divorce their wives by saying to them that you are to me like my mother's back. After this declaration, the husband would be exempt from all conjugal obligations, nor would he have to support and provide for his wife and children. The woman would also be prohibited from remarrying anyone else. She could be put outside of the home and prohibited from making a livelihood to support her children or herself. This was prohibited once Islam came. The expiation for such an offense would be for the husband to free a slave:

> And those who abandon any of their wives through *zihaar* and then would recall what they have uttered, they may free a captive ere they touch each other; that ye are admonished (to conform); and verily God, of whatever ye do, is Well-Aware... (Quran 58:3)

SLAVERY WAS NOT A RACIAL INSTITUTION

Unlike slavery in America, in the Muslim world, slavery was applicable to any party that took a military stance against the Muslims. As Islam produced Muslim converts well outside of the Arabian Peninsula into Europe and Africa, captives of war, of both European and African descent were taken during military campaigns. Despite their ethnicity, these captives were often freed and given the opportunity to obtain powerful positions in government. For these reasons, slavery in the Islamic world could never be compared to slavery of the West.

Slavic and Turkish slaves that were used for military purposes during the reign of the Caliph Mu'tasim from 832-842 A.D. are good examples of non Arab slaves rising to obtain power. These slaves were known as the *Mamluks*, which was Arabic for *those who are owned*. To show the extent of equality between the races in the Islamic world, it would be worth mentioning that from amongst these Eurasian slaves was Muhammad Ali, who founded the first independent Islamic dynasty in Egypt. There was also another group of Eurasian slaves, primarily of Turkish decent known as the *Seljuks*. They served the *Ghaznavids* in Persia, where they eventually formed a state of their own. In a relatively short period of time, these slaves ousted most of the Arab and Persian rulers from their positions of authority in the Middle East. These former slaves and their descendants then dominated the military and political structure in the Middle East for nearly one thousand years. The most renowned dynasty formed by these descendants of military slaves was the Ottoman Empire. Amongst the latest and most prominent of these rulers who were of Eurasian descent was King Farooq of Egypt. He was ousted from his position in1952 and later exiled from Egypt. He was succeeded by Jamal 'Abdun-Nasser, who was the first Egyptian to rule Egypt since the time of the Pharaohs.

The ascendancy of slaves to positions of authority in the Islamic world is an example of how race is not a prerequisite for leadership in Islam. *

THE ARABIC WORD FOR NIGGER: A WESTERN INFLUENCE

The common use of the word *'abd* (slave) towards blacks in the Arab world can give a false perception that Islam is a racist religion. This word is the

---

* This is contrary to the West where more emphasis was placed on Barak Obama's color during his campaign instead of the soundness of his policies.

English equivalent of "nigger." Considering that Islam is wrongly assumed to be just an "Arab" religion, the line is not clear to many whether this is just a word used by some Arabs or something Islamically acceptable.

In America, slavery being exclusively for blacks came from the Judeo-Christian scriptural premises. Likewise, it was gradually introduced to the Islamic world by the West. The evolution of the Arabic word *'abd* (slave), which derives from a verb meaning to *serve*, mirrors this social evolution in the Middle East, as explained by Professor Bernard Lewis in his book *Islam in History*:

> In early classical usage, *'abd* meant s*lave*, irrespective of race or color; by the high middle ages, its use is restricted to black slaves only; in later colloquial Arabic, it is used to mean blacks, whether slave or free.[3]

His reason for this change is that those of African ancestry were more visibly detected as being of non-Arab descent when Islam spread by conversion. Therefore, it was easier to distinguish those blacks who were most likely descendants of slaves; whereas, those who were descendants of European slaves were able to blend in easier with the Arab peoples.[4]

This "may" have played a significant role in the evolution of the word; however, there are other factors to be considered. The first is that Islam supported the abolition of slavery. Therefore, people were to be "slaves of Allah", and not for other people. As an act of devotion to God, people would often—and still do—select names that meant "servant of Allah", by prefixing one of many of God's attributes with the word *'abd*. If someone wanted to call himself the *servant of Allah*, he would add the word *'abd* to Allah, forming the name *'Abdullah*.

The honorableness of the word 'abd was compromised as the Islamic Empire spread into the Judeo-Christian governed nations of Europe and North Africa. It was there that Muslims encountered Jews and Christians where they were influenced by the Biblical belief that servitude was the true destiny for black peoples.

After the discovery of the New Worlds, there was a dramatic change within the European power structure. European nations such as Spain, England, and France became powerful due to their unlimited amount of natural resources and slave labor. The Islamic nations that once dominated science, mathematics, and international trade began to look towards the West as the new leaders and providers of technology, crops, and even social ideologies. It was through this world-wide, economical influence that the West was able to export their racial ideologies, just as if they were sugarcane or cotton.

The fact that the word *'abd* is not defined in any Arabic dictionary as being a black person is evidence within itself that this is merely a colloquial/street corner expression. It is also not defined as so in the Quran or in any of the *ahadith* (traditions), which confirms that this is an innovative expression that has snuck its way into the vocabulary of *some* Muslims. It is no more than a trendy way to appease the Europeans. The Persians resembled this when they changed the name of their country from Persia to Iran to reflect their Aryan ancestry when the Nazi party was extremely powerful in the early twentieth century. Therefore, one cannot define Islam as being a biased religion because of some social trend that some individuals have adopted which is actually in contradiction with Islam.

SUDAN DEBATE

Not only are certain trends misinterpreted as being part of Islamic teachings, but many socio-economic divisions and rivalries as well. For example, despite the availability of Islamic media coverage, most Americans do not choose to rely on it to learn about Islamic issues. Conflicts in the Islamic world in places like Darfur are presented to Westerners with tainted un-Islamic propaganda. Certain media outlets have portrayed light-skinned Arabs killing and enslaving black Africans as if it was a sport.

Journalist, Sam Dealey, a former editorial page writer for the *Asian Wall St. Journal*, clarified many misconceptions about this conflict after spending time with the Janjaweed militia. The Janjaweed have been commonly defined as a government supported, light-skinned Arab group which has unjustifiably killed blacks. Dealey's encounter with the militia's leader, Musa, writes, "Mr. Khaber's group is made up of Arab and African tribesmen. A dark-skinned Berti African, Mr. Khaber describes himself as an Arab."[5]

The Berti people are classified by ethnographers as a black African people indigenous to Africa. The Pan-African organization of Justice in Africa has also recognized the misrepre-sentation of this conflict in a July 30, 2004 report:

> As journalists are finding out when they visit Darfur, it is rarely possible to tell 'Arab' from 'African' by skin color. Most Darfur Arabs are black, indigenous and African. They are 'Arab' in the old sense of being Bedouin, rather than hailing from the Arab homelands of the Nile Valley or Fertile Crescent, and their Arabism is a relatively recent political construct.[6]

American views of conflicts are based off American experiences that usually have had an element of racism behind the clashes: black slavery, the Native Americans verses the white settlers, the slave owning Confederates verses the abolitionists of the North, the Allies verses the white supremacist Nazis, etc. However, Darfur's problem stems from the fact that it is a region that is suffering from ecological degradation and scarcity, and not race.

The region has been affected with devastating droughts over the last forty years, causing the desertification of the land at an accelerated rate. The regions severe droughts and famines have reduced the various groups into a state of desperation, forcing them to compete with one another for crucial necessities. These droughts have caused a severe famine and a massive displacement of groups; nomadic groups gradually moved to the south where they rivaled with other sedentary groups for grazing and water resources. The disputes intensified with the breaking down of once-effective tribal judicial systems and the proliferation of weapons. The western backed Sudan People's Liberation Army (SPLA) used this turmoil to disperse small arms to certain ethnic groups to expand their front on the larger civil war that already existed in other regions.

In order to counter such groups it is widely believed the Sudanese government began supporting nomadic tribes referred to as the Janjaweed as a counterinsurgency. This was a route believed to have been taken in order to avoid a direct confrontation with these anti-government groups. This militia support is compared to the U.S. support of both the Mujahedeen in

Afghanistan during the Soviet invasion, as well as the Contras in Nicaragua who fought against the Sandinista, procommunist government.

Although this conflict can be compared to other conflicts throughout the world, preying on the Darfur issue is a Western political strategy. Sudanese officials expressed that American politicians falsely defined the conflict as a race war and genocide so that the U.S. can mend its image of bigotry and be seen as "liberators" of black peoples. In turn, this would result in African American governmental support. Sudanese Foreign Minister Mustafa Othman Ismail, In a July 2004 interview with the London-based *al-Sharq al-Awsat* newspaper stated, "The only explanation to this escalation is that it has become part of the American election campaign to attract Black voters."[7]

Furthermore, the Sudan is the largest nation in the continent of Africa; it is one of the fastest developing nations in the world due to its exportation of petroleum. "Divide and conquering" means that America can play the role of liberator and "manage" their natural resources as they have in other oil rich countries such as Iraq, with Kurds, Sunnis, and Shiites. Although the war in Iraq stemmed from a lie that Saddam Hussein had weapons of mass destruction, millions of Iraqi civilians were murdered in the name of democracy and freedom. We must look at the Sudan as another potential Iraq: a country that will easily be devastated and robbed if people continue to believe the lie that Arabs are killing blacks legally in Sudan, and that giving them American "freedom" will resolve their problems.

NATIONALISM

Nationalism emerged originally in the Islamic world as a secular European ideology. It was then adopted by the Islamic nations, whose national identity and independence had been suppressed by foreign rule and imperialism during the early twentieth century. Political leaders such as Kemal Ataturk of Turkey and Michel 'Aflaq of Syria revolutionized Middle Eastern politics by discarding the Islamic system of governing and replacing it with a more Western mode of legislation and government. This new system was implemented to salvage the politically stagnant Middle Eastern nations which "appeared" to be ineffective to serve a steadily advancing, modern society.

The main and probably most influential of these Islamic governments to become transformed by nationalism was the Ottoman Empire.

The Ottoman Empire lasted from the 14th century until 1922, when it was established as a republic. It was named after one of its early leaders named Osman ('Uthman). The Ottoman Empire began in what is now modern day Turkey and spread throughout Europe in the 1400s, conquering the Byzantine Empire. At the peak of its reign during the 16th and 17th centuries, the empire covered North Africa, Egypt, Syria, Yemen, Mesopotamia, the Persian Gulf, Palestine, the Caucasus, Azerbaijan, and parts of Europe as far as Vienna and Hungary. The Empire was ruled by a Sultan who governed by Islamic law, permitting other religions to exist under their rule. Each group under Ottoman rule had a leader who would represent its people before the government. After the 17th century, the Ottoman Empire steadily declined until its ultimate collapse in 1922. By this time it had lost all of its foreign territories outside of Turkey.

In Turkey, Kemal Ataturk, played a significant role in introducing nationalism to the Muslim world.* After his victory against the Greeks in the devastating battle of Sakarya, the Grand National Assembly bestowed upon him the title of "Ghazi," which was Arabic for "conqueror." In 1935, Turkish citizens were legally required to adopt a last name. Therefore, in an attempt to publicly declare his nationalistic sentiments, Mustafa Kemal dropped the Arabic title "Ghazi" along with the first name Mustafa, which possessed an Islamic connotation because it was one of the names of the Prophet of Islam, Muhammad (ص). He then selected the surname Ataturk, Turkish for "father of the Turks", forming the name Kemal Ataturk.

This was only one of many tactics used to abandon Arab/ Islamic customs and to "Turkecize" their nation. On November 25, 1925, under the leadership of Kemal Ataturk, the Grand National Assembly passed a law forbidding anyone from wearing the fez or any other brimless hat that reflected Islamic affiliation. These brimless hats were worn by Muslims because it allowed their foreheads to touch the earth when praying—a religious requirement. The premise for Islamic disassociation was based on the reality that Islam is a religion that transcends all geographical and racial

---

*   He was formerly known as Mustafa Kemal when he was appointed commander-in-chief by the Turkish Grand National Assembly in August 1921

barriers. It would be a blatant act of hypocrisy to advocate nationalism (a politically correct term for racism) in the name of a religion (Islam) that clearly opposes such an ideology.

The Ba'th Party (Resurrection Party) was also instrumental in the spreading of nationalism in the Middle East. The Ba'th party began as a Syrian political party formed in 1953. It came into existence from the merging of two political parties. The first was a socialist group led by Akram al-Hawrani. The second group was based on Arab unity and nationalism led by a Syrian Christian named Michel 'Aflaq and a Syrian Sunni Muslim, Salah ad-Din al-Bitaar. Together they formed the "Arab Socialist Resurrection Party," known in Arabic as *"Hizb al-Ba'th al-Ishtiraaki."* The party was built on three basic principles: socialism, liberation, and the unity of Arab peoples.

As mentioned, Michel 'Aflaq brought the aspect of Arab unity to the party. Michel 'Aflaq, born in Damascus, Syria, learned the concepts of racial unity and nationalism as a student in the Sorbonne Academy in France. He was amongst many other Christian Arabs who campaigned for Arab nationalism because it was an idea based on culture and race rather than religion.

The Ba'th Party is still the political party that rules Syria; it ran Iraq until Saddam Hussein was ousted from power. The party is still based on Arab unity and nationalism instead of Islam. This is because the parties have been traditionally run by people who stemmed from minority religious groups that would have otherwise been outnumbered in elections due to a lack of representation. Therefore, nationalism became the cement that was to hold the various Arab groups together.

Nationalism was also implemented in Iran by Muhammad Reza Shah to counter Soviet and British aggression. In 1935, during the rise of the Third Reich in Germany, Muhammad Reza Shah changed the name of Persia to "Iran" to place an emphasis on the Persian's Aryan ancestry. The word "Aryan" is a general name given to an ancient group of Indo-European languages that Persian (Farsi) once belonged to. Aryan, was also the name that the Nazis designated for their "white race" that they deemed superior to all others. Therefore, changing the name of Persia to Iran was viewed as a tactic used by the Persians to appease the once powerful Germans, and to convince them that the Persians would make worthy allies against the Soviets and British—in the name of Aryanism.

However, as in the cases of Turkey and Syria, this idea of nationalism and race superiority was foreign to the Persian citizens, who were primarily Muslims. As time elapsed, the Iranian citizens formed a grass-roots Islamic movement led by the late Ayatollah Ruhullah Khomeini. Due to political corruption under the Shah's rule, this movement seized power from Muhammad Reza Shah in 1979, exchanging the ideologies of Aryanism and nationalism for a theocracy that benefited all citizens.

Nationalism was adopted by any people who sought to liberate themselves from the imperialist powers. They fought back by using the oppressor's tactics to liberate themselves, fighting fire with fire. Furthermore, none of these aforementioned Islamic nations existed until Western powers undermined the Islamic empire that extended across three continents; they were all part of the same Islamic Empire.

BLACK NATIONALISM

In America, Africans had been exploited through the slave trade for 246 years. Slavery was abolished in 1865, only to be replaced by prisons, segregation, and Jim Crow laws. Christian lynch mobs running rampant in the densely populated black South, along with poor economic conditions, caused Africa Americans to migrate to the northern cities in large numbers. There, African American Christians formed their own organizations that aimed to counter the injustices meted out to them by their Judeo-Christian oppressors.

African Americans were introduced and often forced into Christianity by their rulers because the doctrine of Christianity was designed to keep its followers compliant with the demands of their masters. African American leaders such as Booker T. Washington, Frederick Douglas, and W.E.B. Dubois worked diligently to create social change and equality. However, the necessary *tactics* to obtain this social change and equality were never adopted by African American Americans. The tactic that was the most appropriate for such a situation was the *demand* for social change, as voiced by Frederick Douglas in his West India Emancipation Speech (1875):

Those who profess to favor freedom yet deprecate agitation, are men who want crops without plowing up the ground; they want rain without thunder and lightning. They want the ocean without the awful roar of its many waters.... Power concedes nothing without demand. It never did and it never will. Find out just what any people will quietly submit to and you have found out the exact measure of injustice and wrong which will be imposed upon them, and those will continue till they are resisted with either words or blow, or with both. The limits of tyrants are prescribed by the endurance of those whom they oppress.[8]

Oppression of African Americans continued well throughout the twentieth century. No one was capable of uplifting them because Christianization taught African Americans to be Christ like, which often meant that they should suffer the same as Christ did.

During the early to mid-twentieth century, dramatic changes occurred within African American political and religious institutions. The submissive and unassertive nature of the church caused them to gravitate towards doctrines that offered a sense of identity and sound solutions to their dilemma of social and economic inequality. Two of the most distinguished groups to offer such doctrines were the Moorish Science Temple, established by Noble Drew Ali in Newark, New Jersey in 1913, and the Nation of Islam, founded by W. Fard Muhammad in Detroit in 1930.

These two organizations consisted primarily of African American Christian converts. Both organizations referred to themselves as Muslims although they looked more towards the Bible than the Quran for guidance. However, the Quran offered passages that specifically addressed the issues that African Americans faced, making such Islamic influenced organizations appropriate solutions:

41. And whosoever defends himself (in avenging) after being oppressed, then against thee there is no way (to blame).
42. The way (to blame) is against those who do injustice unto the people and transgress in the earth unjustly; these for them shall be a painful chastisement. (Quran 42:41-42)

Although the Nation of Islam never orchestrated a military campaign against the United States government, they possessed the courage to assertively "voice" the demands of African Americans:

1. We want freedom. We want full and complete freedom.
2. We want justice. Equal justice under the law. We want justice applied equally to all, regardless of creed class or color.
3. We want equality of opportunity. We want equal membership in society with the best in civilized society...[9]

Although the Christian minister, Martin Luther King, was the more "acceptable" lead figure in the Civil Rights Movement by the mass media and white Christians, it is a fact that the civil rights bill was not passed until the Nation of Islam was at its peak of popularity in the 1960s. The Nation of Islam was able to inspire African Americans to *demand* equality and justice which actually led to the support of such Christian civil rights leaders as Martin Luther King.

Although the Nation of Islam used the word Islam to describe the religion that they followed, their ideologies and organizational structure mostly reflected their Christian and even Masonic roots. For example, the Quran is specific when it comes to the oneness of God:

1. Say: He, God, is One (alone).
2. God, the Needless,
3. He begets not, nor is he begotten.
4. And there is none like unto Him. (Chapter/Surah112)

The Nation of Islam taught that Master Fard Muhammad, who revealed the teachings of the NOI, was indeed, "God" in the flesh, in the same manner that Christians taught that Jesus was also "God" manifested in the flesh. In Islam, Muslims are commanded to perform congregational prayers on Fridays (The Quran ch.62); whereas, the Nation of Islam congregated on Sundays like Masons and Christians. The place that Muslims pray in is known as a masjid (Arabic for a place of prostration): the Nation of Islam called their place of prayer a temple as the Masons do. In fact, Minister

Louis Farrakhan himself openly declared that he was a Mason at the Million Family March held in Washington D.C. in 2000.[10]

Traditionally, the first step to becoming a Muslim is to declare "There is no god but Allah (س), and Muhammad (ص) is his Messenger." The NOI rarely referred to the Prophet Muhammad (ص), born 570 A.D., as they did Elijah Muhammad, who they considered their Prophet sent from God. With such speeches as *In Christ All Things are Possible, The resurrection of Jesus,* and *The Crucifixion of Jesus: the destruction of black leadership,* the Nation of Islam was able to appeal to the African American Christian community.[11] Despite the resentment that the NOI had against the traditional American social structure, they much more resembled their Christian oppressors than the Muslims of the more orthodox sects of Islam. Their appearance, structure, and dress code, which included clean shaven faces and tailor made suits with bowties, gave them an appearance that was very much acceptable for a church, Masonic temple, or even corporate America. The one they believed was God in the flesh, Master Farad Muhammad, was just as white as the portraits of Jesus created by those Christians that they claimed were oppressors.

The NOI also restricted its membership from white people whom they often referred to as devils. Just as white Christians portrayed their Lord and Savior Christ as a white man, the NOI taught that the black man was the true and living God. Like so many other countries that were under Judeo-Christian domination, the NOI also resorted to nationalism and racism as a tactic to unify black people who were the victims of oppression. Just as the Muslims in the Middle East learned the ideologies of nationalism and racism from their Western rulers, so did African Americans. As Muslims in the Middle East experimented with Turkish, Persian, and Arab nationalism, African American Muslims were the pioneers of Black Nationalism. In each circumstance, nationalism was to be a vehicle to propel a specific group of people against external forces that deemed themselves racially superior. Surprisingly enough, it was a counter strategy that did produce successful "temporary" results in terms of countering racism, despite that it was considered "un-Islamic" to many Muslims.

The NOI is defined by many as an Islamic form of Christianity that emerged from a Western society obsessed with racial purity and segregation. Therefore, it was not the Quran or Islam as revealed by the Prophet

Muhammad (ﷺ) that inspired their racial views, but the Biblically inspired Western nations, who have professed these beliefs that date back to the time of Noah (Gen. 9:25-27), and continue with the Hebrews (Israelites) who were recorded as a superior race of people (Math. 15:16-21). Black Nationalism in the name of Islam was more or less a reactionary movement to "Christian" racial oppression and the root to much of the rivalries in the Muslim world today.

COLORS AND THE BLUE EYE FALLACY

Just as the Ku Klux Klan used Biblical verses to validate their claim that whites were superior to all other races—in the name of Christianity—Black Nationalists used both the Bible and Quran to contend that the Black race was, indeed, God's Chosen People in the name of Islam. These nationalists contended that whites were actually blue-eyed devils on the authority of the Quran that reads: "(On) the day when the trumpet shall be blown and We will gather the guilty ones, and the blue-eyed ones (20:102)."

To claim that whites are those who the Quran is mentioning would be a clear contradiction to the just nature of the Quran. The Quran is understood by *tafsir* (explanation/commentary). The most authentic and sound form of *tafsir* is to use the Quran to explain the Quran. The explanation given by one's own personal opinion is the least accepted form of tafsir. History has proven that laws of any land can be interpreted and applied according to one's own personal interest because of the ambiguity of language. For this reason, a judge must exist to determine if the law is applicable in the case. The Quran is the best of all judges.

The linguistic usage of colors plays an almost identical role in Muslim countries as it does in the West. If I wanted to ask someone "how are you?" in the Iraqi dialect of Arabic, I would say *"shoo loonak?"* which translates as *"what is your color?"* This is because color is defined as a mood or a state of being in the Arabic language. It is similar to how "being depressed," can also be expressed as "having the blues" in English.

Furthermore, when the human eye is afflicted with a visual impairment such as cataracts, there is often a film or discoloration that forms on the sclera and gradually moves inward, surrounding the outside of the cornea.

This discoloration forms around the outside of the cornea, which covers the iris and the lens of the edge. This layer that covers the cornea often appears blue, or blurry. Therefore, being blue-eyed in classical Arabic was to be in a state of blindness, just as asking someone what their color is, is an inquiry to their state of being. Those who turned from the Quran were considered blind (blue-eyed) because they could not see the truth. However, they would be raised on the Day of Judgment in this same state: "And whoever turns away from my monition, verily his shall be a life straightened, and We shall raise him up on the Day of Judgment, blind (20:124)."

To also refute any claims that the Quran vilifies white people, it is worth mentioning that the Quran has verses that vilify the color black as well: "And on the Day of Resurrection thou shalt see those who have uttered lies against God, their faces shall be blackened; is there not in Hell an abode for the proud (39:60)?" Therefore, if those who have blue eyes are a cursed people, then so are those who are black. This is an idea that the Quran is clearly opposed to (49:13).

It is logical to conclude that African Americans attempted to counter centuries of being Biblically sanctioned inferior by reinterpreting the Quran to sanction whites inferior to blacks. There is no recorded history within the traditions of the Prophet Muhammad (ص) of any discrimination or condemnation of any race. For anyone with a basic understanding of the Arabic language and the Quran, Muslim or non-Muslim, it has always been clear that the Quran was revealed to implement equality in society, not to create social divisions.

LEADERSHIP

Anyone who exemplifies justness and their ability to be an effective leader can hold a position of authority in Islam, despite their ethnicity. For those who have spent their entire lives in a country, where positions of leadership are monopolized by one race, it may be hard to perceive a multiracial society being ruled by those of African descent. However, the Muslim world has a long history African leadership.

From amongst the earliest converts to Islam was the Abyssinian (Ethiopian) slave, Bilal—also known as the third pillar of Islam. He was severely tortured and punished by his pagan Arab slave masters because of his monotheistic beliefs. The Prophet Muhammad (ص) then purchased Bilal and granted him his freedom. Bilal then joined the ranks of the Muslims where he was appointed as the *mu'azzan* (the caller to prayer). Bilal also participated in military and political expeditions alongside the Prophet Muhammad (ص) himself. The Prophet was reported to have said on several occasions. "The Muslims should obey their appointed ruler, even if he is a maimed Abyssinian (black) slave."[12]

In fact, the second caliph, Umar bin Khattaab, who ruled the Islamic Empire shortly after the death of the Prophet Muhammad (ص), was of Abyssinian descent. His father, al-Khataab, had an Abyssinian mother.[13] Another prominent leader in the Islamic world of Abyssinian descent was the famous general Amir ibn-al 'As, who conquered Egypt and was one of the great architects of the Islamic Empire.

Other leaders of African descent include Ya'qub Ibn Yusuf, also known as al-Mansur. He ruled Morocco from 1149-1189 and invaded Andalusia twice, rising to become one of the greatest of the Moorish rulers of Spain. There was also Ibrahim al-Mahdi, the black poet and musician who became ruler of Syria in 686 A.D. and was elected some 25 years later as the caliph of all of Muslim Spain.

There was also Imam Musa al-Kaazim. His father was the well-renowned descendent of the Prophet Muhammad (ص), Imam Ja'far as-Saadiq (ع), founder of the Ja'fari (Shiite) school of thought. His mother was Hamiida Khatuun, a Noth African. Imam Musa Al-Kaazim is the seventh holy Imam of the Shi'a, born 745 A.D. (128 A.H.). He has a magnificent shrine which still stands today in a suburb of Baghdad named after the great leader (al-Kazimiyya, Iraq). His son, Imam al-Ridaa, is the eighth holy imam for the Shi'a who also has an exquisitely embellished shrine in Mashhad, Iran. The shrine is visited by devout Muslims from all over the world who pay tribute to the deceased ruler, who himself had a Nubian mother.

Even in contemporary times, dark-skinned Muslims of African descent have held prominent positions of leadership in Islamic heterogeneous societies. A very distinguished figure was the late Egyptian president, Anwar al-Sadat. His mother was Sudanese and his father was an Egyptian. According to American standards, he was considered a dark-skinned black man. However, this did not dissuade the citizens of Egypt from supporting his presidency of the most populous Arab nation in the world.

Initially, Sadat was welcomed by many Egyptians as a president who presented himself as a devout Muslim and sincere leader. He was also commended by the Muslim world because of his military victory over Israel in 1973, where the Sinai Peninsula was reclaimed by Egypt. However, Sadat had a disastrous, western supported, capitalistic, economic program known as the *Infitaah* (the opening). It was extremely unpopular amongst the Egyptian masses. His political and economic gravitation towards the United States, along with the peace treaty that he made with Israel, is what had led to his assassination. Corruption was acknowledged as being widespread in his administration, and was reported to have reached his family circle.[14]

The manner in which he has been reported to have exploited the Egyptian people was compared to that of a monarch, a pharaoh to be exact. According to reports, the leader of the four assassins that killed Sadat shouted, "My name is Khaalid al-Islambuli. I have killed Pharaoh. I am not afraid to die."[15]

In Quranic Arabic, the word pharaoh and *malik* used in reference to tyrannical or oppressive rulers. The Arabic word for king is *malik*; however, the word malik is only used in honorable and orthodox way when it is used as an attribute of God. The first chapter of the Quran refers to God as *malik yaumi diin* which is *the king of the day of judgment*. In Islam, *Malik* is usually prefixed with the word 'abd (servant) which would construct the name 'Abdul Malik (the servant of the King/God). The word malik (king) is referred to negatively in the Quran when used towards *people* where the Queen of Sheba exclaims to Solomon that, "Verily kings when they enter a town (victorious), ruin it and make the noblest of its people the meanest; and thus will also do (Quran 27:234)." Likewise, the word Pharaoh is used negatively when applied as a human attribute: "And came Pharaoh and those before him and the cities overthrown, with evil. (Quran 69: 9."

Therefore, it was the oppressive Pharaoh-like atmosphere of Sadat's administration that led to his assassination, and not his race, which was confirmed through the testimony of the leader of Sadat's four assassins who stated, "I have killed Pharaoh."[16]

THE FEAR OF ISLAM

History shows that there have only been two conquests on Europe by non-whites that had significant influence on the lives and culture of Europeans—the Moors and the Ottomans. Both groups were Muslims. People may make reference to Hannibal and the Africans that accompanied him during his conquest of Europe; however, compared to the 400 year old Ottoman Empire and the almost 800 year rule of the Moors in Spain, Hannibal's 15 year occupation of Italy was merely a short lived military campaign that left no significant influence on European culture, language, or its infrastructure. Western nations are fully aware of this, which explains their true fear of the spread of Islam.

Across the board, Black leadership is more common under the folds of Islam than under the Judeo-Christian religions because of the lacking of the Hamitic/African curse of servitude. Furthermore, the Judeo-Christian religions do not "specifically" have scriptures that indicate that Africans are suited for leadership. Islam is extremely clear where the Prophet Muhammad (ص) stated, "The Muslims should obey their appointed ruler, even if he is a maimed Abyssinian (black Ethiopian) slave."[17]

Western leaders want to distort the true nature of Islam through media outlets to make it appear as though it is an oppressive and evil religion to frighten people. With the majority of people terrified of Islam, many will not even consider approaching it as a medicine for their social dilemmas, but will falsely identify it as a poison. This means that those who are in power through usury, discrimination, and ensnaring many into various traps, will rest peacefully on the premise that most will not even investigate to see if there is any validity in what the media professes to be the truth.

CHAPTER 7

The Answer

One of the biggest obstacles to overcoming our social problems is that many "experts" have been consumed in identifying the problems, but failed to propose effective, realistic solutions. Since society is made up of individuals, individual change is the key to a much broader social revolution. Therefore, the following chapters are dedicated to offering simple Quranic steps that anyone can follow as an individual to counter the aforementioned social problems.

Anyone can use these concepts despite their race, age, or geographical location. There is no money that has to be paid for a service, or a product, only a simple reflection on these ideas and a realistic, honest attempt to apply them.

The solutions are a combination of seven principles based on Quranic verses that were the most prominent and effective in diffusing the issues addressed in the first half of this book. They also brought success to the Muslims that I interviewed. I will not repeat boring sayings and clichés, or just quote the Quran, because many people do this and still can't resolve personal issues in their own lives. In my approach, I elaborate off of the Quran and offer personal experiences and share unique interviews that illustrate the application and power of these principles, which are:

Self Building
- ✓ Reeducate Yourself
- ✓ Realize That You are in an Economic Jihad
- ✓ Be a Leader
- ✓ Redefine Yourself

Interactive Goals
- ➢ Maintain Family Relations
- ➢ Avoid the Traps
- ➢ Accept the Oneness

These principles are in direct accordance with the Quran, and I believe that many people have not attempted to do what I've done out of fear of being called an innovator by unsuccessful, negative minded, ignorant critics. The reader should remember that even the Quran gives examples of the Pharaoh, the prophets, and situations to help convey its principles; therefore, I use a similar approach to understand the Quran.

The first four strategies (1. Reeducate Yourself, 2. Realize That You are in a Economic Jihad, 3. Be a Leader, and 4. Redefine Yourself) are personal tactics that should be perfected in order to make the individual stronger and prepared to venture out and confront the obstacles in society. The last three (5. Maintain Family Relations, 6. Avoid the Traps, and 7. Accept the Oneness) are designed to assist in dealing with society. These principles are based on interactions with others which comes after mastering the first four principles of self development.

CHAPTER 8

Reeducate Yourself

O' ye who believe! If cometh unto you a wicked man with a news, ascertain carefully, lest ye harm a people in ignorance, and then repent ye for what ye have done. (The Quran 49:6)

The beginning to overcoming social obstacles is through "bridging the gaps". This requires knowledge of yourself and others. As I travelled to different masjids to conduct interviews, I noticed that Many African Americans and Palestinians would socialize after Jumah and discuss business and politics. Many of the African Americans were very empathetic to the Palestinians situation and would even quote what happened back in 1948 and the unjust UN policies that were placed on the Palestinians but not the Israelis. Likewise, many Palestinians could relate to African Americans. On several occasions I heard Palestinians quote Minister Louis Farrakhan on subjects like Zionism. I've met about a dozen people named Jihad. All of them were either African American, Palestinian, or Iraqi, which showed me that struggle was an integral part of their culture. There seemed to be more empathy between these groups than amongst Muslims from autonomous nations like Morocco, Egypt, and Pakistan who were sympathetic, but not so much empathetic and understanding of their cause, which they often had a hard time relating to because they never experienced it personally in their own nations. People from these nations tended to identify with certain things that white Americans could identify with such as independence day, which is a reality for them, but just a goal, or even a fantasy, for Iraqi Shiites, Palestinians, and African Americans. I believe this is why the name Jihad is common amongst Palestinians and African Americans, but rare, or only used as a *kunya* (nickname) in autonomous Muslim nations.

Likewise, I noticed that in Shiite masjids that wherever there were a large amount of Iraqis there was a significant amount of African Americans. I attribute this to the fact that many African Americans can relate to the commemoration of Ashura: the remembrance of the martyrdom of Imam Hussein, the Prophet's grandson, an integral part of the Shiite ideology. He died on the plains of Kerbala standing up to an oppressor (Yazid). Most ceremonies include crying for the Imam who was killed along with 73 of his followers who stood up to an army of tens of thousands. Many African Americans can relate to this on the grounds that their own struggle seems to be equal to his as far as the "odds being stacked against them."

If empathy allows these different ethnic groups to unite then we must all implement empathy in our lives to form sincere unions with others: listening and watching them when they speak, paying close attention to what they say and how they say it, and doing research on the cultures and experiences of others.

Likewise, immigrant Muslims that want the West to understand them have to understand the West. They have to understand the history of the different ethnicities that form this nation from "their" perspective: Latin Americans, Irish, Italians, African Americans, etc. Until you can develop a real empathy and knowledge of others you can't expect them to do the same for you. I also realized that many of the American Muslims that said that they were victims of racism didn't speak any foreign languages and had little knowledge about the cultures of the people that they said were discriminating against them. The people that were offensive also had no understanding of the people that they were harming.

I speak Arabic, English, and Spanish. In almost any environment I tend to be the one that people are more willing to open up to because they feel comfortable with someone that is familiar with their culture. I'm usually able to help them gradually abandon their stereotypes. Likewise, I don't assume people are sitting around and conspiring against me all day when they speak a foreign language because I either understand their language, or I understand that people speak about the same thing in their languages that we do in English, which is usually nothing. Through learning about others we learn more about ourselves, because we approach their way of life and compare it to our own, eliminating the "this-is-how-we-are" concept and replacing it with "this is how people can be."

* * *

I met Rdwon at the Lake City Islamic Center in Northern Florida. What struck me about him was that he broke all the stereotypes of a Muslim from an Arabic speaking country that many westerners have. Although he is Arab by language, he would be considered a dark skinned black man according to American standards. His children play with the other children in the masjid. His son, Rafiq is an exceptionally good basketball player. His wife socializes with the other women from Pakistan, Bangladesh, Palestine, and other nations in the masjid's eating quarters after salaatul jumuah. His family participates in all the events with a diverse group of people where no distinguish is made between race.

Rdwon struggles to deal with the same thing that most immigrant Muslims that I interviewed faced: being labeled as a terrorist. It seems as though September Eleventh has scared the memories of most Americans with the images of jumbo jets crashing into the two largest economic centers in U.S. history. Since then, there have been numerous reports of Muslims being discriminated against by airport officials, where anything associated with Islam in an airport raises a red flag. Rdwon is not only amongst those Muslims that denounce what "Al Qaida" did that day, and using airplanes as weapons to kill Americans, but he actually works as an airplane technician, ensuring the American passenger's their safety.

My interview with him was brief; however, he was a source other than the media that could speak about the Sudan conflict from a black man's perspective who lived in Sudan during the conflict.

RDWON RAFFAY

I'm from central Sudan. I went to a university back home and I graduated from Westwood College here for aviation. I speak Arabic and English. I've been in the United States almost 7 years. A Sunni Muslim. I work at Temco as an avionics technician dealing with electronic systems on airplanes.

Life in the Sudan

Life in Sudan is simple. Some people have rich lifestyles, others are not so well off, but the majority just live a simple life. Some tribes raise cows, others raise camels, or lambs, then, you have those that farm crops. Most of the country does agricultural work. In the central region we do the farming, we have big irrigation systems (like any advanced country). In the west, north, and south people raise livestock (camels, goat, and sheep) because how the land is. But in the east, they raise camels because it has big desert and it's dry. They can survive better there.

Sudan War and Racism

I'm not a refugee, but I won a lottery to come to the United States. I'm not sure about exactly what is the cause behind the war. But I do know, from the media, that it's tribal, and there is a lack of water and grass. And there is no development in that area (Darfur). Everyone in Sudan is affected by the war. Because if I'm not affected directly, a lot of money is directed towards the military for war that stops it from circulating amongst the masses.

In Sudan we do not classify ourselves by color like in the United States. Nobody even asks you what tribe you belong to, unless you get official paper work like ID or a passport. You can tell what tribe someone is from their name or their accident.

I belong to the Jumuwiya tribe. It's an Arab tribe, but we are mixed with African. Basically, we are African, but our culture and language is Arab. For example, the Janjaweed's roots are Arab, from the Middle East, but they mixed with the Africans, but their culture and their language is Arabic. A long time ago they came from Arabia through the Sinai down through Egypt and mixed with the African peoples. So, today, the people in Sudan are mixed.

Sometimes a person may use the word *abiid* when they're mad, like cussing. In Sudan the word *"abiid"* (slave) is not commonly used. It is used towards darker skinned people in other countries. During the eighteenth century the British came and took the black people and sold them. But before their arrival *abiid* was used only when someone was caught in war and they were taken as a prisoner. It was used for anybody, black, white, any people.

Conclusion

I wish that everyone in America would treat people the way that they would want to be treated. The American people need to get closer to know the true Islam. After September 11th they have a bad understanding of what Islam is really about. Islam is about respect. Everyone is equal.

I wish I could convey to the people that Islam is different than what the media displays. Islam is not about killing. Islam means peace. I'm Muslim, I'm not bad, I'm not here to kill anybody.

* * *

In order for me to see if the concept of Universal Brotherhood was actually being practiced I had to not just get its verbal profession, but its realization and capture it being practiced in real life. I visited the Islamic Center of the Lehigh Valley in Whitehall, Pennsylvania unannounced during Isha prayer on a Monday night on July 27, 2009. I had never visited the masjid before, and no one knew who I was or what my mission was. I chose Monday because it is not mandated for Muslims to attend the masjid as it is on Friday. Therefore, a Monday would attract the Muslims whose devotions exceeded beyond the mandatory minimum requirements of the religion.

There were about a dozen Muslims from different nations such as Egypt, Malaysia, Pakistan, white Americans, and others. Not only did they find away to offer the evening prayer at eleven at night, but they stayed around to participate in a Ta'leem (Islamic study) afterwards. After I introduced myself to several people and explained my project, I was directed to Waseem Akhtar who was in charge of their interfaith program.

* * *

Waseem Akhtar is a children's doctor. Originally from Pakistan. He has lived in Philadelphia and New York prior to living in Allentown, and has been in the United States for 15 years. He is the director of the interfaith program at the Islamic center in Whitehall, PA. The program meets with different religious groups and educates them about Islam from a Muslim perspective.

*At first he was a little reluctant to answer questions. I assumed this was because he didn't know me. There was a little tension in the beginning of the interview. He became more comfortable after I opened up about the personal stereotypes that even some of my family in the North have about their own blood relatives in the Sout*h.

WASEEM AKHTAR

Solutions to Overcoming Prejudices
I would like to educate the American people on Islam. So far, the only source of information that is used about Islam is the media and the media has not portrayed a true picture of Islam. What the media does is just take some of the actions of some Muslims and portray that that is what Islam is. And that is where the disconnection is. I would like to make sure that people knew the genuine Islam to make a distinction between the actions of the people and Islam, to see if the action is Islamic or non-Islamic. In our interfaith meetings we teach people the basic Islamic principles and tell them that these Islamic principles will help you distinguish between what is Islamic and what's not, and then you can decide for yourself.

Marriage and Segregation in the Muslim World
I think that there is a fear of the unknown. You know your people and know your culture, you don't have to do an experiment if you marry your son or daughter within your own people, but with anyone else outside of your culture or community you're doing an experiment. There's always the fear of the unknown. So, when I'm embarking myself on a journey where I don't know the destination I'm always fearful. So, there are people that would make those choices, but they are doing it with caution. So, I don't think that anyone is comfortable doing it unless there is some motive behind it. Like if somebody falls in love, then they are not thinking about anything else except love, so they are okay with that. But as a parent they're not in love with that guy or a girl. They are still thinking in an objective way. The motive for the two people getting married is love, but for the parent, the only motive is that my son or daughter is happy on a long term basis. So, people don't know the consequences of intercultural marriages or how to

deal with it. Maybe that's the reason that many people don't do that (marry across cultural lines). Even in Pakistan people don't usually intermarry. They stay within their own culture and own people, communities, and clans, and languages. You always see exceptions here and there, but they're not very common. It's about a comfort level. When you get comfortable with something you don't want to change it. Change is not easy.

Summary
I think that I got here without any discrimination. It probably is happening, but if I have come here and I have gotten what it is that I deserve, then probably things are working. So, whatever is happening it is productive. There's always room for improvement. I do hear that some groups and some communities think that they are discriminated against racially, but it's really hard for "me" to say, because I'm an example of coming here from outside and I did not see that happening. And everything happened on merit for me. I think it is working fine, but it may need improvement, and if there are some exceptions then I think they need to be addressed.

* * *

Reeducation as a Solution
When thinking of famous explorers, Marco Polo, the Venetian, is one of the first names that comes to most people's minds. However, Ibn Batuta, a North African Arabic-speaking Berber, traveled three times as far as Marco Polo and lived during the same era. Ibn Batuta (1304-1369) was also an author whose book *Rihlah* (Travels) is an important source for the history and geography of the medieval Muslim world. He traveled 75,000 miles, reaching Spain, China, Timbuktu, and the Steppes of Russia.

Another historical omission is the origins of much of the science and technology of today. Algebra, the basis of most of our advanced forms of mathematics, is actually named after Jaber ibn Hayyan (721-815 A.D.), an Arab Muslim and chemist. Amongst his many great works was the earliest recipe for nitric acids and innumerable other contributions that lead to the development of chemistry. There was also Avicenna (980-1037), also known as ibn-Sina, an Arab Muslim. He was a poet, an astronomer, a philosopher, and a physician. He authored *Canon of Medicine*, which was used globally as a medical text for 600 years. His major philosophical work, *The Cure*, displayed his interpretation of Aristotle's philosophy; it had more influence on Western thought than any of his other works.

Despite these great achievements of Arab Muslims, many in the West have been programmed to associate Islam with destruction and primitiveness. Some people even make it their duty *not* to learn so that they can continue hating and justifying the wrongdoings of themselves and their nations through ignorance (as if not knowing exempts them from guilt).

Solutions to Reeducation

If we want to make an impact on the opinions of others, we should consider reaching out to the youth before their opinions begin to form. Thomas Pettigrew, an expert social psychologist at the University of California at Santa Cruz, who has studied prejudice in depth for about half a century describes, "The emotions of prejudice formed in childhood, while the beliefs that are used to justify it come later. Later in life you may want to change your prejudice, but it is far easier to change your intellectual beliefs than your deep feelings. Many Southerners have confessed to me, for instance, that even though in their minds they no longer feel prejudice against blacks, they feel squeamish when they shake hands with a black. The feelings are left over from what they learned in their families as children."[16]

Kyle "Kamal" Burton, an African American New York City fire fighter expressed:

> The one stereotype that I have to deal with is that all black men are lazy. How could I change people's views? That's the problem with most racists and "people" in that matter; even if a person's views are different from the stereotype that they have in mind it still doesn't change their views about the masses. It's like you say one bad apple spoils the bunch, one good apple doesn't make the bunch good. It's still "he's the exception." That's what they look at. So, no matter how hard you work, a racist mind doesn't change his views based on one person's actions, or two people's actions, or three people's actions, or a hundred people's actions. It doesn't change. It's in them, it's inbred. They say you can't change

any one's mind once they believe in their heart what it is they believe. So, if they truly believe that I'm beneath them, then, no matter what it is that I do, they are going to feel that I'm beneath them. No matter how hard I work, no matter what I do to try to change their minds.

I met a man in Washington D.C. of Bangladeshi descent at Masjid al-Islam named Muhaafiz married to an African American woman. He said, "I grew up in Prince George County in Maryland which is predominantly black. I know what African Americans go through." Muhammad Latif, a Caucasian Muslim from Valdosta Georgia, who runs an urban-wear store with an African American Muslim and Egyptian said, "I grew up in Egypt. Being white was hard. The kids used to call me Hawaga which meant an occupier after the British. I know what it's like to be a minority. That's why I can understand African Americans so well." Growing up in an integrated environment allowed the two to be void of the prejudices that are common in the world, because they carry their childhood experiences with them.

The benefit of reeducation from the victim's standpoint is that you have an understanding and mastery over the person who is discriminating against you or prejudging you. You can also eliminate the idea that the person is discriminating against you. Many people believe that Muslims are prejudice because there are not a lot of ethnically diverse marriages; however, as in the case of Doctor Waseem Akhtar, he explained that even in Pakistan, people stay within the clans that they feel comfortable with, the same way that southerners or northerners in America might click together out of comfort.

When you are treated unfairly, discriminated against, or wrongly prejudged you can either become offended and hurt where a sense of defeat overcomes you, or you can understand the other person's side which is people "know what they know." You can't let your emotions be dictated by the actions of uneducated ignorant people, which is what I've seen a lot of people do: resort to alcohol or drugs, violence, anger, or some other negative action to cope with the social obstacles they face such as job discrimination or police brutality. These "choices" lead to one's own destruction such as legal problems, high blood pressure, heart attacks, and other health related problems. In the case of Islam, it is only natural that non-Muslims who are hit continuously with anti-Islamic propaganda all day to respond negatively when they are confronted with Muslims.

However, it's the job of the Muslim to select a strategic approach to dealing with these types of people:

1) Reeducate that person to eliminate their misconceptions: your intentions and motives for taking a particular action, the truths about religious or racial groups, enlightenment your won background and lineage, or whatever is possible to eliminate their fears.
2) Reeducate yourself about others to clarify any misconceptions that you may have. Furthermore, understand the source of their prejudices.
3) Forgive them for their ignorance. Holding grudges can lead to insanity.
4) Use your own strategies.

Knowing Others is to Master Them
Kyle "Kamal" Burton made studying other people work for him to deal with the obstacles that he faced for being both a Muslim and an African American, trying to coexist with other fire fighters in the white dominated New York City Fire Department:

I've studied others, where they've not studied their own, and they're following blindly, and if they ever took the time to study their own they wouldn't study, follow, or lead the way they do, because they accept things on blind faith. It comes to the point where I say "you know so much, well tell me something about Islam to explain why you hate it?" And they can't tell me anything about it. "Oh, Muslims are terrorists." Do I look like a terrorist to you? You don't know anything about me. So how can you pre-judge me? You don't even know anything about my blackness. But I know about you. I'm the X-factor, I'm that unknown variable, and they're trying to figure me out, where I'm not trying to figure them out. I wouldn't say that I know them, but I know more about them than they know about me. I took the time to read their books (Christianity). I took the time to learn their lessons, and to speak to them, when they never took the time to speak to me. So, when I make my preconceived notions about them, I'm basing them on experience. What are they basing their hatred and stereotypes on? What they read in the newspaper? What mommy and daddy taught them?

Whether you are a victim of racism and stereotypes or you possess them yourself, the first step to overcoming this barrier is through "reeducation", as the Quran states: *O' ye who believe! If cometh unto you a wicked man with a news, ascertain carefully, lest ye harm a people in ignorance, and then repent ye for what ye have done.* (The Quran 49:6)

CHAPTER 9

Realize that You are in an Economic Jihad

O Children of Adam! Look to your adornment at every place of worship, and eat and drink, but be not wasteful. Lo! He loveth not the wasteful people. (The Quran 7:31)

Give the kinsman his due, and the needy, and the wayfarer, and squander not (thy wealth) in wantonness. (17:26)

Being financially secure and having more than just enough to live off of is insurance against oppression. Some people may say "I'm content with just enough to survive on. As long as I have food on the table and a roof over my head, I'm okay." But what if the police stop you one day as your going home and discriminatorily charge you with something that you didn't do? If you're poor, you can't even afford adequate legal representation. For someone just content with survival, the roof over their head and the three meals that the department of corrections will provide them with should be enough to meet their needs.

To not be a victim of oppression means to avoid being dependant on others, because you are put in a position where you can be treated harshly and unjustly. Some may argue that is the natural consequence of living in the ghetto or being African American; however, there are many African American Muslims that have used Quranic principle to help lift themselves above economic barriers that others in their same position can't.

I visited a masjid in Jacksonville, Florida which was almost 100% African American. During the Friday sermon, the imam stressed the importance of having your own business. The risk factor, which stops many from taking the venture, was addressed as well. His answer was that even if you break even throughout the process you have succeeded, because you created a salary for yourself and for others. During a time when unemployment is a crisis, they have done the impossible—employed the unemployable. Needless to say, there are over one hundred businesses that are operated by worshipers of that masjid. This makes them one of the most powerful and independent communities within the state of Florida. They are less likely to be victims of racism or oppression because they are self sufficient and economically secure. However, their successes were a result of strategic planning.

Just as drinking alcohol, cursing, and smoking cigarettes are vices that are hard to break because they are habitual, so is spending. It is more of a challenge for the poor person that has grown accustomed to spending all of his money in order to pay for necessities than someone that has always had an excess of wealth, who is in a comfortable enough position to utilize it for more than just primal necessities. When there is finally an excess of wealth, the poor person usually "finds" something to spend it on simply because he has never had an opportunity to save and has it fixed in his mind that money was made to be spent instead of saved or invested. This practice is most common during income tax time. As a manager of a store, I've seen two sisters buy werewolf contacts and a list of other frivolous items with their income tax checks who, just a week prior, complained to me about the terrible situation of the economy and that they had barely enough money to survive.

I saw this same trend in South East D.C. as well, where people stepped out of their rickety housing projects owned by the government, and stepped into new cars with rims as they wore thousands of dollars of jewelry. It's not just in D.C., but a national trend. In fact, African Americans are the largest consumers out of all ethnic groups. However, Imam Abdul Alim Musa's community (Southeast D.C.) is an exception to the rule. They own their masjid and several properties in the area. Even if the recession continues, they will not have to worry about being homeless. They can simply pay the property taxes. They are free of "slave" interest. Although they face the same economic hardships as others in their neighborhood, they were obviously happier than the others, which I attribute to the better understanding that they have of how society operates and the role that they must play in order to maintain their economic and social independence.

Washington D.C. is one of the most economically oppressed areas in America. Within its ghettos lay Imam Musa's community that has created a peaceful neighborhood that has an almost Southern hospitality. They own their own masjid and several properties in their neighborhood. Although many people argue that you can't buy a home or property without getting in debt and taking out a loan, Imam Musa's community paid for every last one of their properties straight out, with no loans.

Just the trip alone to their community was a learning experience. Coming from New York City for other interviews, I felt comfortable driving through Northwest D.C. The streets were well paved, the lawns were manicured, and the people seemed to have something constructive to do. By the time I got to North East D.C. I realized that it was a different world. There were detours on every other street due to all of the road construction which made finding Masjid al-Islam extremely difficult. I asked several people for directions to its location on Benning Road, but everyone was paranoid and walked away nervously with expressions filled with suspicion—like most people would when confronted by a stranger in a high crime neighborhood. There was trash in the streets and steel bars over the store front windows. The row houses reminded me of Philadelphia or Baltimore. I could tell unemployment was high because there were a lot of people hanging out, looking around with nothing to do.

I finally made it to Benning Road which was a wide Avenue with factories in some spots, other areas were flooded with barber shops, nail salons, and pop up mini malls that are common in the rest of the country. As I got closer to the masjid there were less buildings, the houses were bigger, and there were more trees. I could see the hardness, frustration, and the inner city anger in a lot of people's faces. Maybe it had something to do with living in a neighborhood that had signs for two bedroom apartments for twelve hundred dollars a month that would probably go for five hundred where I lived at in Florida. Or maybe the answer was in the boarded up gas stations which reminded you that it is a roll of the dice whether your business is going to survive or not. Once I arrived there, Imam Musa gave me good insight on how to devise a good economic plan. He reminded me that it requires patience, careful spending, and a collective communal effort in order to succeed economically.

* * *

Imam Abdul Alim Musa was born in 1945 in Arkansas. Imam Musa grew up in Oakland, California where he associated with H. Rap Brown (Imam Jamil Al-Amin). He went to Algeria in the sixties with other exiled members of the Black Panther party such as Eldridge Cleaver. He embraced Islam during a time when the Nation of Islam was at its peak of popularity. He is an orthodox Muslim who Mirrors the Nation's "do for self" motto.

He is now the Imam and director of Masjid al-Islam in Washington, D.C. and a member of the Institute of Contemporary Islamic Thought (ICIT). He is the founder of the Islamic Institute for Counter Zionist American Psychological Warfare .He is also the director and founder of As-Sabiqun which means the "vanguard" of Islam. As-Sabiqun is an Islamic movement that is trying to create the circumstances that will lead to an independent Islamic state in North America by 2050. The organization is built on Quranic ayahs such as:

"O ye who believe! Stand out firmly for justice, as witnesses to Allah, even as against yourselves, or your parents, or your kin, and whether it be (against) rich or poor: For Allah can best protect both. Follow not the lusts of your hearts, lest ye swerve, and if ye distort (justice) or decline to do justice, verily Allah is well-acquainted with all that ye do." (The Quran 4:135)

Ye are the best of Peoples, evolved for mankind, enjoining what is right, forbidding what is wrong, and believing in Allah. (The Quran 3:110)

ABDUL ALIM MUSA

Interest

In order to expand a community you have to be able to have your own schools, your own property, and your own stuff. Other people aren't going to give it to you. They're going to be too demanding. They're going to water down your lines and your mode of operation. You can do it, but it takes a good strong pool of families working together. You can succeed without resorting to *ribaa* (interest), but you have to really be tight (with spending). Now, they have different schools of thought that allow a person to buy "one" house on *ribaa*, but they can't go into real estate; like say now, real estate is cheap, and a person couldn't go and borrow money (to buy property) to become rich. It doesn't allow that, but it allows someone to buy one house because when you are paying rent you are paying someone else's *ribaa* anyway (mortgage). To live absolutely "ribalessly" it's going to be difficult.

Even the Yahud (Jews) of today lend and borrow. At one time it was prohibited for them to do so, to charge each other high interest rates. But now everybody is doing it. The Zionists don't practice Judaism, but the Hassidic Jews practice it from the torah.

Do For Self
(Now as far as convicted felons succeeding), most brothers that I see start their own businesses. They're not going to get a job in a corporation; they don't even have jobs for college graduates and straight and narrow white folks. If they have a low skilled job they will usually give it to a Latino at a lower wage. Someone illegal or something like that. The answer is self sufficiency. We have to do it by ourselves.

There isn't any system that is going to help us work this out, and I don't think that there is any group of Muslims that's going to help us either. We have to do it ourselves. We got to start with nothing, penny pinch; you got to have a tight crew. A person is not going to make it too well on his own. That's why we're so strong on community building. Because sooner or later a guy is going to hit a rough spot and he's going to need help. And no matter how well off he becomes, he can take one step and stumble and fall altogether to the gutter—economically, *if* you don't have community. That's why Islam stresses jamaat. The solution to all of these things is a strong community. I mean "real" community.

You have to build that because they don't exist. And, you have to have patience, because the police are going to send so many snitches in to mess up your business. If they know you're going to help a good Muslim, then they are going to send the police to borrow up all the money. They'll borrow it and go bankrupt: "I can't pay it back" (the borrower will say). So, I can't help nobody else. They're going to do that. You got to be a miracle worker almost.

Realize that You Are in an Economic Jihad
We make it, but we got to fight for everything. You can't take any setback as a setback. These are some serious times. There is no smooth way that I can think of. I don't see any. It's going to be very hard, very tough.

I'll give you an example. We just cleaned out a house that we have a few blocks from here. We let a family of "Muslims" move in because they were being kicked out of where they were; we don't do that first month last month rent. So, they moved. Now, we just remodeled the place, it was about 15, 20 thousand to remodel it. They did about $25,000 in damage to the place. Purposeful damage. To live like that it is by design. Then, they stopped paying rent about a year ago. Being brotherly, we let them go. We don't want to be like a business about it. Finally, they just popped up and left a few days ago. We went around to clean it out, and it's going to cost us about another $20,000 to get it back up to par.

My estimate is that they are on the government payroll. Since we *do* own property, they try to send snitches and informants to minimize the gain on our property. To burn our wealth. Like if some good person is coming for help they'll jump in the front of the line. That way, the money will never get to the good needy Muslims. It will get to pretending Muslims, who are actually government agents, who are getting in line in order to waste our resources. So, it's not easy.

Whatever happens we are thankful to Allah. If a person is going to do good in the United States or anywhere else with Muslim dictators or whatever they call themselves all over the world, hey, man, it's a good time for struggle. That's all I can say. If your name is Jihad that's what time you're living in. An economic Jihad, a social Jihad, and every other type of jihad you can name.

I did a lot of time in the pen, but I had to come out and start from scratch. Here in Washington D.C. if they have a program to help one felon they got ten programs to help the rich. D.C. is a plantation. You got to struggle no matter where you go. Especially when you're talking about Islam. Most of the Muslim groups and organizations here are controlled by the government. That's why you never get any help by any so called good Muslims who are able to help. They're stooges themselves.

CHAPTER 10

Be a Leader

And when it is said unto them, "Come unto what God hath sent ye down unto the Apostle," say they, "Sufficient for us is what we found our fathers upon." What? Even if their fathers knew nothing and were not (rightly) guided? (Quran 5:104)

Because man has been created to follow what he believes to be the norms of society it is very easy to be swept up in whichever way the current is flowing. Certainly, this is a tremendous ankle weight in man's race towards forward progression: following the crowd.

As an author, the concept of leadership has a deep importance to me; I believe that no words could actually capture its true value. I began to really analyze the simplicity that came with being a follower when I think back to the first major league baseball game I attended in Queens, New York. I was twelve years old and watching the "World-Series-champions-to-be," the New York Mets, playing against the Atlanta Braves. I sat quietly in awe at the sight of the tens of thousands of fans and the fact that I was in eyesight of professional athletes like Darryl Strawberry, Dwight Gooden, Gary Carter, Keith Hernandez, and Mookie Wilson. Shortly into the game I watched the fans jump up from their seats on the end of the stands on my far left and form a human wave. As this wave of excitement approached me I sat there puzzled, wondering what its purpose was. I sat there more interested in the game than joining in with the drunk, off-duty executives, city workers, and others jumping out of their seats yelling out grunts and sounds that only a caveman could understand. I was amazed that adults that I had always perceived to be so well-mannered and refined would jump up and yell to form this human wave that led to nowhere and seemed to have no purpose. I actually thought they were a little "crazy."

Nevertheless, after about the third time that the wave came in my direction I threw my hands up in the air and yelled unintelligibly with the best of them. I was commended for my display of "fan solidarity" by a redheaded Irishman sitting behind me. He rubbed the top of my head like I was his little puppy and said, "That's the way to go!" I paid my dues and became accepted as a true fan.

The point being made is that it's easy to get swept into the crowd. Acceptance is a fundamental component to our human composition. There was no harm done from participating in this human wave; however, the question is "what do you do you do when the crowd is wrong?" Can you take your own course when the ways of the crowd are harmful to your own development? Do you submit to your inner desire to be accepted?

These are difficult questions to ask, especially when there is an emotional connection between the individual and the group to be followed. The love of family, race, or community can make it a painful ordeal to tell the group you won't follow their habits or ideals. This refusal is almost always interpreted as a rejection of those individuals instead of the "act" that is being abstained from. It may come from amongst criminal minded youths who may wish to shun one of their long time friends because he doesn't want to steal or do drugs. The same applies for family members that may want to use the younger generation into the same corrupt lifestyles that they themselves followed (as a legacy of those who came before them). Usually, a denial to follow in their footsteps leads to a complete separation. Only a strong minded person can muster up the courage to be independent and to accept the isolation from that which he or she loves in the pursuit of forming a healthy, prosperous life.

Leadership is not just standing on a pulpit with a suit on making promises. When I say leading, I mean to take the initiative to be in control. This may seem hard for people that might be disenfranchised felons, whose life experiences make them think that someone will always be pushing the controls in their lives. For example, a lot of people that I met coming out of prison have lost voting rights, some even permanently. I met a Muslim named Sabir in that situation from Norfolk, Virginia who said, "I sent Obama fifteen dollars for his campaign. I can't vote, but I got something just as powerful." And as we know, Obama raised more money for his campaign than his opponent did. I've also learned that people can come up with innovative strategies for solving their own economic, domestic, legal, and financial problems, by dealing directly with the opposing parties rather than depending on an outside institution to resolve the matter. Realizing that you don't have to be dependent on the system is power. A dependant mind is a slave's mind. Leadership is placing personal affairs into your own hands.

Not only does leadership require breaking away from the crowd, but also being able to lead one's self and others. Leadership requires power: of will and wealth. In order to make change, being in a position of power and influence is mandatory. If you don't like the way that your community, family, or society is in, then lead them in a different direction.

* * *

Shaikh Saed Ali Kulayni was born in and Harlem and raised in Queens. He now lives in Atlanta and is a manager at a Wal-Mart. He was 33 at the time of this interview. I chose Saed Kulayni for his leadership qualities. He is an African American Shiite sheikh (Islamic clergy). Traditionally Shiite Muslims have been associated with Iranians, Indians, and Pakistanis; that's what made him unique and why I chose him as an example of being a leader. Unlike most African American religious leaders who tend to be restricted to leading their own communities as pastors and ministers, not only does Saed Kulayni lead African Americans, but numerous ethnic groups. At his masjid I got to see that there were Blacks from the Caribbean and America amongst Iranians, Pakistanis, Iraqis, Moroccans, Caucasians, and many others, where not one ethnic group dominated the other. I conducted the interview at "Aladdin's", an Arab restaurant in Atlanta, Georgia in 2009.

SHAIKH SAED ALI KULAYNI

I've been Muslim my whole life. I was born in Harlem, New York, raised in a middle class neighborhood in Queens, New York and later on lived in the Bronx. I lived in Rego Park, Queens on the other side of the Expressway from Lefrak City until I graduated from High School. I knew a lot of people from Lefrak from school that were into that life (the streets), but I chose to ride skateboards and bikes. Some of my friends were Spanish, some of them were Philipino, Egyptian, Jewish; we all just hung together, it wasn't just one type. So, I never had a problem dealing with people. As a Sunni I was introduced to the Jafaria school (Shia) from my older brother. Then I started to do my own research through the Sahih sita (six authentic tradition books) and it led me to becoming shi'i.

I used to hear a lot about the Arabs not liking African Americans growing up. A lot of times they would go to an Islamic Center and the people would look at them funny, but I came to realize that people do that because you're a new face and they want to see who you are. Me myself, I never came into contact with any type of racism outright. Every community in which I've been to I've never had problems. I do my worship and I leave. I go for *salaatul Jumah, Duah Kumayl,* and any functions that they have during the year. I've never had any problems. Is it the way I look? I don't know. Maybe it's the way that I carry myself when I'm in regular clothing. People tend not to categorize me as belonging to a certain group or being a certain type of person.

When I come in with my *amama* (turban) or *abayah* (cloak) a lot of times people will ask me where I studied or for how long because of who I am. It's not bad, but there are just not a lot of black sheikhs. There are a lot of black sheikhs in Africa and in London, but there's not a lot like you see in other nationalities (Iranians, Iraqis, Indo-Pakistanis) where it's just natural. I was looking at something on Shia Channel or one of these other channels and this guy was saying, "Has anyone noticed that there are a lot of black sheikhs these days." And basically what he was saying was am I the only one that noticed this, as if they are just starting to pop up out of nowhere. So it's something new that you see, black shia sheikhs. I guess they're intrigued and they want to know more about us. I don't think it's anything about racial profiling, or you can't be a sheikh because you have a dark complexion, or because you're of African descent. I think it's just interest, something new.

I was in Canada some years ago at a conference, and there were a lot of other sheikhs that didn't speak Arabic. I'm qualified to perform an *aqiqah*, the *eid* prayers, funerals, the *jumah* sermon and the prayer. From *aqiqah* to *janaza* and everything in between. Actually I get more calls to give lectures from the immigrant community than from the American community.

Leadership
I know most African Americans are Sunni, but just because the majority is the majority doesn't mean the majority is right. Just like having a saying for many years, thinking that it's correct because everybody said it, then you find out that it's something fabricated, a lie, something that just wasn't correct, but all these years you believed this. Why? Because so many people said it. Just because so many people follow the four schools doesn't mean that their views are correct, and mine are wrong.

Islam came as a guide. Rasuwl Allah (ص) came as the physician and Islam is the medicine which the Muslims are the patients to take. We go to the Rasuwl Allah (ص) and the Imams—the physicians. Islam came to cure the evil that's within man. To help man be guided right. *Allah (az wa jal)* gave us the tools to live righteous lives.

Islam itself is against oppression. Oppression is worst than slaughter. A tradition says "Those that don't practice *amr bil maruf and nahya an al munkar* (enjoining what's right and forbidding what's wrong) is like a corpse that is dead, but perceives to be alive." Another tradition says that if you don't practice this a tyrant will end up ruling over you and prayer alone will not help you. So, we have to constantly practice these things. Certain things you can't allow. Oppression is wrong. Why should you oppress your fellow man? Why should you stand for this, being oppressed? Do you think it's correct? If somebody tries to oppress you, do you accept it? No, you shouldn't. You should always enjoin what's right and forbid what's wrong.

Family
Family has played a big role in my life you can't cut ties with your family; you have to keep that relationship. My family supports me, and whatever I want to do they support me. It's never an issue about what I want to do. Work is worship, and you have to support your family.

If I don't work, I can't go to Hajj, pay *zakaat*, *khums*, or enjoin in what's right and forbid what's wrong.

When I'm enjoining in what's right, I'm making sure that this money is being earned in a *halal* way, and given back to the needy people. Money is important because it helps many when it's spent in the right way. If I work I can sponsor the *iftar* and feed the people during Ramadan, send someone to hajj or *umra* and all of these extra things. Work allows me to keep a roof over my head, food on my plate, and my family happy.

It was ironic that Sheikh Kulayni brought up that foreign Muslims were intrigued with him. As we were on our way out the door a Saudi Arabian man approached him and asked him the same questions that he mentioned in the interview: his origin, where did he study, etc. The man's first question was "are you a Muslim?" The sheikh answered, "Why else would I be dressed like this?" (motioning to his one piece Islamic garb). He ended the comment with a laugh. Within seconds, the sheikh made a new friend.

CHAPTER 11

Redefine Yourself

That man can have nothing but what he strives for... (The Quran 53:39)

Our destination is often determined by our perceptions of ourselves. The child groomed to believe that his or her worth is high will most likely lead a life much different than the child who is continuously neglected and degraded. The same applies for the boxer who has a charismatic trainer in his ear telling him that he is a tiger and he's going to devour his opponent. He will most likely do better than the boxer who is discouraged by his coach who is always hinting that he should throw in the towel before he gets demolished.

Similarly, groups of people are often labeled and treated in certain ways that contributes to the direction that they will lead. We may not realize it, but we often fall into the stereotypes of the socio-economic group that we fall into: certain ways of speaking have become the "white" way or the "black" way of speaking or thinking. In some cases people may do things that they believe are cultural requirements, but contradict their ethics. I've met Muslims from certain countries that may beat on themselves during religious events to mourn for the martyrdom of a holy figure. When I ask why do they do it, the usual answer is that it's culture. It's a fact that the one they say they follow (Prophet Muhammad) never did this. Despite its negative perception and the fact that there are more ways to benefit society while expressing themselves, this practice continues although it is pre-Islamic, and considered un-Islamic to many.

If there is a negative label that one selects, the action of the individual may reflect that attribute through their actions. Breaking these negative trends requires the personal pursuit of learning the "unseen" realities of the circle that one belongs to in a light different from the one showed on the big screen to rake in money for Hollywood. This is when "redefining" one's self comes into play. This means to either place one's own definition to the label that one lives under, or to rid one's self of the label altogether.

For one, many of the labels that we live under are not those chosen by ourselves, but names created and forced upon us by the ruling class. As in the case of race, this was done to form a racial caste system. The ruling group took titles that reflected greatness in order to secure power and to secure their legitimacy as rulers. In many cases these inaccurate and often offensive titles were given to those who had been reduced to submission and did not have the power to disagree.

When the early settlers first arrived in America they assumed that they were in India; therefore, they named the Native Americans accordingly: Indians. Even these Native Americans were given names and subdivided according to the settlers wishes as in the case of the Sioux of the Midwest. The name Sioux actually comes from the Ojibwa (Chippewa) word for them, translated into French by early explorers and traders as Nadouessioux ("adders," a kind of snake, used in the sense of "enemies"). This term was reduced to Sioux and passed into English. The Sioux generally call themselves Lakota, Dakota, or Nakota, meaning "allies." Despite the fact that the word Sioux is offensive these people are still referred to as the "Sioux" (the Snakes), and this continues to be their official legal name; there still exist a Sioux City, Iowa, and a Sioux Falls, South Dakota. It is worth mentioning that the "Sioux" live under the worst socio-economic conditions known in the United States.

Bombay, India was named by Portuguese settlers. The word Bombay came from "bom bahía" which meant "good bay" in Portuguese. However, the Indian government changed the city's name to Mumbai in 1995, which is a name indigenous to the Indian language. Likewise, the word "Puerto Rico" means "rich port" in Spanish. This is what the European settlers saw when they explored the "new world": rich ports and good bays. They gave these names to these locations and peoples according to the roles that they were to play in their bigger empires.

This also holds true with racial classifications. Notice how words such as black and white are defined (*The American Heritage Dictionary*):

white (hwīt) n. *Abbr.* Wh. .... 4. A. Having the comparatively pale complexion typical of Caucasoids. B. Of. Pertaining to, characteristic of, or dominated by Caucasians. C. *Slang.* Fair or generous; decent. Usually used ironically: *That was very white of you!* 5. Not written or printed upon; blank 6. Unsullied; pure. 7. Habited in white: white nuns...

black (blăk) *adj.* **blacker, blackest** *Abbr.* bl., blk 1. Being of the darkest achromatic visual value; producing or reflecting comparatively little light and haven no predominant hue. 2. Having no light whatsoever: a black *cave.* 3. Belonging to an ethnic group having dark skin; especially, Negroid. 4. Dark in color or having parts that are dark in color. Used with animal and plant names: black bass; black birch 5. Soiled, as from soot. 6. Evil; sinister: *black deeds.* 7. Cheerless and depressing; gloomy. 8. Angered; sullen. 9. *Sometimes capital.* B. Attended with disaster; calamitous: *the stock-market on Black Friday.* 10. Of or designating a form of humor dealing with the abnormal and grotesque aspects of life and society and evoking a sense of the comedy of human despair and failure. 11. Indicating or incurring censure of dishonor: "Man...has written one of his blackest records as a destroyer on the oceanic islands," Rachel Carson. 12. *Informal.* Absolute; confirmed: *a black villain...*

Although many people have tried to glorify and redefine the word *black,* its negative usage dating back to Biblical and Quranic times outweighs the good applied to it through the American black legacy that deals with important eras, historical events and figures, inventions, etc. In fact, the word *black* is defined worse than the word *nigger,* which has a vague definition, meaning merely a derogatory word:

nigger (nĭg´ər) *n.* Vulgar. A negro or member of any dark-skinned peoples. An offensive term used derogatorily. [Earlier English dialectical neeger, neger, from French *nègre*, from Spanish *negro,* NEGRO.]

Universal Brotherhood: Quranic solutions to overcome racism and oppression

Groups such as Moorish Americans (Moorish Science Temple and others) have acknowledged the title black for what it is—a derogatory term forced on a group of people to form a racial caste system—and referred to themselves according to their true ancestral identity—Moors. In reality, *black* is a word coined by pink people to define bronze, copper, golden, and mahogany colored peoples, so that a racial hierarchy could be formed. It is not what people are, but what they are forced to classify themselves as.

Moorish Americans associate themselves with the Moors that once ruled Western Europe (Spain) for over 700 years. They don't believe that they have to carry the label *black* or represent the role that has been written by the oppressors. Instead, they associate themselves with greatness, and as the Moors that once ruled Spain, they understand that they also have the same potential to rule over Europeans, right here in America.

However, some people are too accustomed to it to get rid of it. They use the title, but at the same time they are aware that the word's definition is not what's in mind when it's being used. It's similar to how we say "sunrise" or "sunset", but in reality, the sun doesn't rise or set; the earth revolves on its axis as it orbits the sun. Kyle "Kamal" Burton, a Muslim NYC firefighter explained:

> You look up the definition of black in the dictionary and it always says something dark and disturbed. How would I define black? Black is beautiful. That was something that I was always taught about myself. How could I look at myself and think of something negative? I can't attribute myself with something bad. If Webster created the definition of something dark and horrible as being black, then, guess what? I can't agree with Mister Webster. I'll show you someone black that's not dark and gloomy.

Furthermore, everyone that I interviewed agreed that the lack of a positive identity was one of the biggest issues which caused many to shed the overall identity of being black. Llewellyn "Naji" Coleman, a Muslim that works as a marketing director in NYC said:

> It's like what I felt about the deen, wearing the Islamic "so called" *sunnah* outfit. Once we get into anything, be it Yahweh Ben Yahweh

(Hebrew Israelites) or whatever, it seems as though we get into it so deep until we have to take on the identity of that thing, because it's like we don't have an identity. Like the Eastern Parkway thing (Labor Day Parade), the blacks from different countries have two flags. They have the American flag; they may have the Trinidadian flag. We fly with what? Just one flag here. It's like we don't have an identity. And when we get into something, we want to start wearing the turbans, we want to, wear the jalabiyyahs; we want to pray so hard that we don't even think about getting a job, which is *haram* (forbidden). And when we get to start thinking for ourselves without somebody telling us what to do, there's anarchy. And this mosque is a big proof of it.

Kyle "Kamal" Burton explained:

The biggest problem is that we lack is identity. You always see that we want to be a part of this group, or that group or we want to fit in with this or we want to fit in with that. What's wrong with fitting in with where you are, or who you are. If you don't like yourself, how can you expect somebody to like you? It sounds strange, but in Islam you see it so much until sometimes it becomes embarrassing. For example, Pakistanis have a culture. But Islam is a faith. It's what you believe, it's how you act. It's a way of life, but there's a way of living it. You don't have to live it the way others live it. You live it the way it should be lived. So, should I dress the way that they dress? If I dress moderate, am I less of a Muslim? Or am I more of a Muslim because I have a dashiki, a kufi, and a long garb on? If I got on that and I'm smoking a blunt as opposed to the brother with a pair of khakis and a regular shirt on who's steadfast in his deen; who's more of a Muslim? But the guy wearing the garb will feel as though he's living the Islamic life. Just because you're wearing that doesn't make you Muslim. We tend to adapt other people's cultures. And I'm like I'm not wearing that; that doesn't look comfortable to me. I can't wear a nice pair of sneakers, with some jeans and a button down?

And that's one of the things I don't understand. There are certain foods that they eat. I mean do I have to eat curry chicken? Can I not be a Muslim and eat fried chicken? I like barbeque chicken. Do I have to eat Basmati rice (Arab rice)? But you find that a lot of Muslim brothers try to adapt that to make that part of their life. Because they feel as though that makes them more Muslim; and I don't get it. How can I expect you to respect me, and I don't even respect myself. How can I expect you to accept my culture when I'm trying to accept yours? I don't even accept my own culture. That's why I say that there are racist Muslims, because they look at you and they laugh because you're trying to be like them. And they're like this is something that I grew up on. Why are you wearing something that's not native to your home land?

The Need for Racial Classifications?

Some argue that racial classifications are important in regards to identification. If this is so, then, why isn't the complexion of one's skin used to describe someone as eye and hair color and height and weight are used on driver's licenses and other ID forms?

Even as used for identification, race classifying is ineffective. There are Americans very dark such as Italians, North Africans, and Indians who place white on their IDs; however, if a news flash would come on television or a police APB, anything but white would be given as a description. The same rule applies for biracial people whose appearance would be closest to classifying them as Hispanic, Arab, or perhaps Italian, but are coerced to accept black as an identity. This is an open display of white supremacy that says "one drop of black blood taints the holy white race", when in reality, they are no more black than they are white.

So, as a form of identification, racial classifications should not be used to identify people no more than religion or zodiac signs, especially considering that there exists and intense ambiguity that prevents any clear way of defining one another in an ever-increasing racially diverse, multi-ethnic world. Racial classification is also equivalent to denying our ties, as if we are of a different species. It is a regressive act, except for those who possess the more flattering titles, and translates into side-taking and rivalry against other human beings. It is a dark cloud for oppressed people in the West, and an ankle weight that prevents people for keeping up with the rest of society. Therefore, we must redefine ourselves in order to make effective change and remember that "man can have nothing but what he strives for (The Quran 53:39)", regardless of the script written for us.

CHAPTER 12

Maintain Strong Family Ties

Then be like ye are, if ye hold authority, that ye make mischief in the earth and sever the ties of kinship! (The Quran 47:22)

O' man! Take shelter in your Lord Who hath created you from a single self and created from it, its pair, and spread from these two, men manifold and women, and fear God, in Whose name ye importune one another, and (be mindful) of kinship; Verily God is vigilant over you. (The Quran 4:1)

    The problem with having weak family ties is that there is no real support network. Many African Americans are now leaving northern cities and returning to the south where they have families and are doing better than they were in the north due to stronger support networks. Tragedies against blacks in cities like New York take place easier because the cities are overly diverse. When an African immigrant is shot to death by the police, or a Haitian immigrant is sodomized in the precinct bathroom with a plunger, the rest of those of African descent look on with little emotional connection between them and the victim simply because they don't feel any connection to that person. People have openly expressed "I'm a Dominican, Puerto Rican, Jamaican, Senegalese, Trinidadian, or American; he's not one of my people." Words like immigrant and the victim's place of origin are skillfully used by the media to assist in alienating the rest of society from having an emotional, ethnic connection with that person to minimize public unrest. However, if these victims had sizeable blood ties in New York, the odds are that these crimes would not continue in the capacity that they do. There would be organized rallies, marches, and boycotts.

The role of family is like the role of a coach during a prize fight. Life is a struggle. It's easy to throw in the towel and quit when you don't have someone on the sidelines watching your mistakes and strong points, giving you inspiration to make it to the next round. Success is not just one person making it, but a group of people succeeding, linked and networked together, where each person acts as a crutch for the other.

Although America has thousands of universities and colleges and has produced millions of "so-called" experts, the general population lives in ignorance. America has thousands of experts on criminal justice and law, but at the same time has the largest prison population in the world. America produces more mental health experts than any other country, but everywhere you turn there are people losing their minds from New York to LA and everywhere in between.

It is not hard to determine what the problem is: a dysfunctional family structure. The western idea of freedom has created a culture obsessed with individualism and selfishness which rarely leads to success. "Doing it alone" means working twice as hard as everyone else to end up with half the results just to say that you are independent.

The world is controlled by families. America is more of a family oriented oligarchy than a democracy. It is run by families: Bushes, the Clintons, the Kennedys, etc. This rule applies to the Islamic world as well, whereas, the center of the Islamic world is named after and controlled by the Sauds—a family.

In the world of business you can see this same trend. Most of the corporate dynasties in America are created or ran by families: Ford, Trump, Tisch, Bronfman, Busch, Marriott, etc Likewise, it was family members that often assisted the founders of these dynasties with wealth or guidance (such as Donald Trump who used his father's wealth to form a small empire). In fact, about half of the *Fortune* 500 largest industrial companies are family controlled.

Sometimes people laugh when I refer to organized crime families to uphold this principle, but in reality, the most powerful and best organized crime syndicates of our era were the Genovese, Colombo, Lucchese, Bonanno, and Gambino crime *families*. No matter what realm you look in, legal or illegal, good or bad, you will see the significant role that family plays when it comes to success.

Family is the oldest institution in the world. Family is an organization that will exist through blood even after the most powerful corporations fold. The commonality of kinship constitutes a love that is unique. It is much stronger than the flimsy ties of camaraderie displayed by sports fans rooting for their favorite team or any concept of patriotism. The love of family creates the purpose to excel and succeed for their sake. Through that strong love, overcoming racism and oppression is a natural process that is involved through providing one another's needs.

Doctor Waseem Akhtar who accredits his success on his family upbringing said:

> My family gave me support from the beginning to the end. To nurture you, to help you grow, to support you while you're going through different phases of life, such as studying., and to make sure that you're successful. And to celebrate your successes. And to get support just to get there. I don't think that without support of your family that anyone can get there. I mean there are always exceptions. That's why we are born in a family, and we cannot live without them.
> In Pakistan we are more closely knitted, the family system still, which maybe falling apart recently, but in my times we lived together, we were very close and had a joint family system. I think that there are benefits to family as far as being together and helping each other, although some people may differ.

At the same time, the institution of family can be a double edged sword. A family that is built on upholding negative traditions will not benefit any of its members. The only way that a family can take advantage of their relationship is by having good values and upholding high standards of living. Secondly, there must exist a sense of nobility that transcends far beyond material possession; meaning, even the poorest family from the lowest socio-economic background can live an honorable life.

This brings me to the following interview of a man that has used his strong family ties to navigate himself through the obstacles that he faces as an African American and a Muslim. Kyle Burton "Kamal Abdul Karim."

***

Kamal was Born in Brooklyn, New York, and raised in some of its worst neighborhoods (East New York and Bedford Stuyvesant). He is 36 years old and has been practicing Islam for 25 years. His mother is African American and his father was African American and half Puerto Rican. He's married and has four children. I chose him because New York City's unemployment rate is at fifty percent for African American males; however, Kamal has three jobs. I was intrigued about how he could maintain three jobs and raise and provide for a household with four children. I was also fascinated about how he, as a firefighter, was able to get a position in the New York City Fire Department, considering that it is almost entirely white male dominated, and has a reputation for being probably the most discriminatory profession in New York City. Also considering that 343 firemen died in the World Trade Center attacks, it is no surprise that he had his hands full overcoming the dissent that his colleagues already had for him being a Muslim.

KYLE BURTON "KAMAL ABDUL KARIM"

Discussing racism is important because Prophet Muhammad (ص) was oppressed at that time. You also have to think about your own racism and oppression that you're dealing with yourself. Growing up in a society that had 400 years of oppression and finally overcoming that, and moving on to other issues of racism. We're no longer oppressed out in the open. It's all done behind closed doors with political or legal agendas.

People look at me and they don't understand where I came from. If I tell them half the things that I've seen or grew up in and done and lived in, they wouldn't believe me because of where I'm at now. How could you not think that? You don't think that it's possible? But it is. Look at half the kids that are living it now.

What made me feel that I could pass the fire department test is that I'm not an idiot. I don't have an extensive education, but I'm smart enough to pass a civil service exam. Plus, when I ran into one of the recruiters, I was kind of leery about taking the job anyway. It was never something that I thought I would do. After speaking to the recruiter, there were a bunch of black fire fighters that were recruiting African Americans to take the test. And most people say "hey, I'm not taking this job, I'm not running into a burning building, but after hearing all the benefits of the job, I said this is something I definitely should be doing.

I have 3 full time jobs. I'm a firefighter I work baggage claim at the airport (Kennedy). I do staffing for a staffing company (catering). I have 3 jobs because of persistence. My father always taught me never to be lazy. So, I didn't have my father most of my life, but from what I remember of my father, he always provided for his family. I have a family I have to provide for. So, regardless of whatever, I have to make sure they have food on their table, clothes on their back, and a roof over their head. So, if it means not sleeping for 3 days or not having a social life, or any life, then that's the sacrifice that we make for our children.

Being from where you come from you always know that your goals and objectives have to be that much higher than the competitor's, because you have a strike against for being African American. You're black and your counterpart is white, basically, you already have 2 strikes against you. So, you have to be that much better, stronger, and faster in anything that they're doing.

As far as me being a victim of racism, where do you want me to start? In my childhood? In my adult life? Where do you really want to begin (he smiles)? Pick an era?

I work for the New York City Fire Department. It's not even diverse; it's predominantly white male until it's probably considered a white male's job. You're fighting for a position that they don't want you to have. It's a family orientated job where you find a lot of cousins, uncles, brothers, fathers, and sons on that job, and somebody's relative didn't get the job that you have, so they look at you as the enemy.

I'm in a (fire) house that's predominantly white. It was considered one of the most racist firehouses in the city (in Flatbush, ironically, a black neighborhood). I was the first black fireman to be assigned to that house in 30 years. For me it was like "wow"! But when you've grown up around racism and being affected by it, it becomes second nature to you. It's not something that makes you feel uncomfortable. It makes *them* feel uncomfortable, because they become more aware of you being there. And knowing what today's society is like, they do have to be a little bit more cautious of what it is that they say around you. The law has changed with racism. There are sensitivity issues that are brought up.

When I first walked into my firehouse I was like "whoa"! (His face tenses like he's bracing for a punch). I'm sure they weren't expecting me to walk through the door. They see the name "Kyle Burton," one of the most typically white names you could find, then they see this black guy walk in the door, and they're like "uh-oh, who does he know?" Either that or "who did we tic off?"

I started (at the fire department) in July of 2002, six months after 9/11. The first question that you get is "why don't you eat pork?" Then you get the million and one questions, then, you get the whispers… That's another part of the whispering that you get used to. Some are able to differentiate between Islam and al-Qaida. You get some who are just ignorant of world politics or world cultures. And that's what you blame it on—sheer ignorance. If you took the time to educate yourself you wouldn't group one into the masses. Or what goes on in Iraq. They look at every Muslim as Saddam Hussein, when half the Muslim population probably couldn't stand him.

The president of the Vulcan Society of the Black Firefighters Association is a Muslim. He's in my Battalion. And there's a masjid right across the street from his firehouse on Foster and McDowell. So, we would go over there and make salaah during Ramadan and break our fast. You should see the looks that we get. A lot of people ask me why I don't' eat pork. I say the bible that you read says you shouldn't eat pork, so why are you questioning me about why I'm not eating pork? I follow my doctrine, why are you not following yours? So, they know I'm very confrontational, and that I don't like to be questioned about anything in Islam. I know something about them that they don't know about themselves. One thing that life has taught me is that you can't follow something blindly. You have to learn and study other avenues before you can follow your own avenue, so you'll know if you're travelling down that right path.

There have been blatant acts of racism that have taken place (in the fire department). For instance, someone once told me that if you shake a white person's hand the first action after they shake your hand is to wipe their hand off. It was something that I didn't notice prior to that person telling me. But it made me cognizant of every time I shook someone's hand to watch what they did after I shook their hand. And believe it or not, it's a common practice; and when you go up to a brother and shake his hand, he's not wiping his hand off. You can walk into a different firehouse and the first thing you do when you go on a detail is introduce yourself. So, I would go and introduce myself (he extends his hand) "hey, how you doing? I'm Kyle...I'm from such and such..." And I'm noticing that (white) guys are wiping their hands off. And I'm like "is my hand dirty or something?" (He frowns). The black guys shake your hand and give you the chest bump, you know, the ghetto handshake. Whereas, now you're like wow! I mean it doesn't happen all the time, but you do see it happen.

But am I not going to feed my kids because of that? Am I going to turn down a great career because of that (prejudices)? No, I'm not. You're going to have to put me out. I'm not going to make it easy for you. That's what I was always taught in life. Don't give in to their ignorance. Because you make it easy for them. They don't make it easy for you, so why should you make it easy for them? They don't want you there; *make* them tell you that you have to leave.

Attributing Family Upbringing to Success
The older generation played a great role in my success because if they didn't knock down the barriers in racism then, I wouldn't be able to do half the things that I can do today. I mean just think about basic education. If they didn't start integrating schools, what type of education would I have? My mother played a very important role in my success because for one my father died when I was eleven, so she raised a boy to a man. There were other male figures in my life that showed other things and taught me a few lessons, but not like family.

My mother sacrificed a lot making sure that we maintained an education, a correct standard of living. She didn't have the best job in the world, but she sacrificed doing that job so that she was there when we left for school, she was there when we got home. She gave up her life, so how can I not give up mine (for my children).

There are a lot of obstacles in being African American in America. The struggles that you face growing up in your neighborhood, seeing the things that you've seen, dealing with the hardships. Those things lead to your character and determine what you become and where you go. Do you fall victim to your surroundings? Or do you try to fight out the urges to not become part of your surroundings?

The Power of Reeducation

I've studied others, where they've not studied their own, and they're following blindly, and if they ever took the time to study their own they wouldn't study, follow, or lead the way they do, because they accept things on blind faith. It comes to the point where I say "you know so much, well tell me something about Islam to explain why you hate it." And they can't tell me anything about it. "Oh, Muslims are terrorists." Do I look like a terrorist to you? You don't know anything about me. So how can you prejudge me? You don't even know anything about my blackness. But I know about you. I'm the X-factor, I'm that unknown variable, and they're trying to figure me out, where I'm not trying to figure them out. I wouldn't say that I know them, but I know more about them than they know about me. I took the time to read their books. I took the time to learn their lessons, and to speak to them, when they never took the time to speak to me. So, when I make my preconceived notions about them I'm basing them on experience. What are they basing their hatred and stereotypes on? What they read in the newspaper, what mommy and daddy taught them.

Parenting

My wife is an elementary school teacher. And one of our biggest debates before she became a teacher was "who's to blame? The teacher or the parent?" She always thought it was the teacher's fault, until she became a teacher. You can say the teachers don't care as much as you want, but it's not their job to care. It's their job to educate. They can teach a lesson, but if that lesson is not being reinforced at home that lesson won't be learned. When your third grader comes home and calls his momma "Pam" and his grandmother "Momma", there's a problem. And that problem is passed down from generation to generation. And this is where it is at now. It's through the effects of slavery, of what they consider genocide. And we don't see these things taking place in predominantly white neighborhoods.

Now, mommy either goes to work, or she can sleep because she was partying at the club the night before. So, the kids are left to fend for themselves. So, in that aspect, the racist stereotype that falls onto our kids is, is that a society issue? Or a racist issue? That has been passed down the generations until this is where it's at now. These are the effects of years and years of slavery, racism, and oppression, things that have been passed down from generation to generation; it's finally reached this point. Now, where does the next generation fall? That's the scary part. You think it's bad now; what happens when those kids who are not being educated reach adulthood? Half the kids nowadays don't have a respect for life whatsoever. So, now they're falling victim to the racist stereotypes—that black kids are nothing but thieves, gangbangers, and killers.

CHAPTER 13

Avoid the Traps

Verily! As for those whom the Angels have taken (in death) while they are wronging themselves (as they stayed among the disbelievers even though emigration was obligatory to them), they (angels) asked them, "In what condition were you?". They replied, "We were weak and oppressed on earth". The Angels asked, "Was not the earth of Allah spacious enough for you to migrate therein?" Such men will find their abode in Hell - what an evil destination! Except the weak ones among men, women and children who were unable to devise a plan, nor are they able to direct their way {35} An-Nisa': 97-98

> 166. *When would those who were followed renounce them that followed them, and they would see the torment and the ties between them are cut asunder.*
> 167. *And those who followed shall say, "O' were there for us a return (to the world) then we would renounce them even as they have renounced us;" Thus will God show them their deeds (which shall be the cause of) intense regrets for them; and they shall not get out of the (Hell) fire. (al Quran 2: 166-167)*

It's easy to fall into traps for certain people that may grow up where they are familiar with the "ins and outs" of crime, where it is not difficult to resort to it to improve your economic situation, simply because they learned it through walking outside of their homes and observed it openly in their community.

The Quran is filled with examples of the pharaoh, the people of 'Ad and Thamud, and others who were destroyed for their arrogant belief that they were above universal truths that all people are subjugated to. These examples are given so that the reader can ponder on them and relate them to his own personal life. Likewise, it's up to the individual to analyze his own personal situation and apply his own solutions to his problems that he understands the intricacies to better than anyone else. Even doctors, with their years of experience and credentials, are commonly sued for malpractice for misdiagnosing someone and doing more harm than good. There is no insurance that comes with advice. No one is going to be compensated if the advice that they followed gave them nothing but misery. The Quran reads:

21. And they shall come forth before God all together, then shall say the weak unto those who were arrogant: "Verily we had been your followers, can ye therefore avert form us any part of the chastisement of God?" They would say: "If God hath guided us, we too would have surely guided you: it is the same to us (now) whether we implore (*impatiently*) or we are patient, (now) there is not for us (any) way of escape."
22. And shall say Satan after the affair is decided: "Verily God promised you the promise of truth, and I gave you promises but failed to keep them to you; and I had no authority over you except I called you and ye responded unto me; so blame me not but (rather) blame yourselves; I cannot be your aider (now), nor can ye be my aider; Verily I disbelieved in your associating me with God from before; Verily shall be a painful chastisement." (al Quran 14: 21-22)

Therefore, it's up to the individual to weigh out his natural talents, desires, and potentials against his external environmental factors to select the best solutions. This is why the principle of leadership is directly related to avoiding the traps. "Getting there" involves a strategic thought process, and not done impulsively without considering long term consequences for a split second decision.

Avoid the Traps

Kyle "Kamal" Burton stated:

I chose to break away from what everybody else was doing because I saw what it did to my family when my father was locked up. I saw what it did to my family when my sister got locked up. It was one of the stereotypes that I wanted to break away from, "that all black men have been in jail," or "headed towards jail." I'm not built for prison, but then again, who is built for it? There are some guys who are hard core criminals, and that's just something that they're into.

Fast money and easy living is always the trap you have to face, because when you grew up in poverty and you are seeing quick and easy ways to make a better living even though it may be short, it's better than what you're living in now. That's always a trap. You never see a retired drug dealer. It's a short, fast life. You end up in one of two ways: dead or in jail.

You're talking about a trap. How about not being able to feed your kids, and this one is saying you can come out and make a few hundred real quick just standing on this corner holding this package for me. That's a trap and a half. Or better yet, let's just go out and rob some cars. A couple friends of mine were car thieves. You don't even have to do anything, just be a lookout. A quick way to make money.

Just knowing that I don't want to be away from my kids helped me avoid that. Going to see my father behind bars. Waking up and not being able to see him in the middle of the night if I needed him. Learning to fight on your own without that guidance of a man pushing you, showing you what you needed to do. Those were the things that helped me avoid the traps. It wasn't based on because I didn't want to. Trust me, sometimes those were the things that helped me get by. You don't know how long you're going to live so you just live for the now like most black kids do. They don't concern themselves with the future because they don't feel as though they have one. You live for the here and now. That's why "I" feel as though so many of the youth *do* deal drugs, get caught up in burglary and things like that, because they feel they don't have a future. I didn't feel that way.

* * *

One of the most entertaining interviewees that I had was Llewellyn Coleman. He grew up in the sixties and seventies, and has mixed a cool swagger from that era with an Islamic personality and character that is upright. Although he is just as familiar with the streets as most people are with their living room, he understands the traps that many people in his age group fell into. He's much more secure financially, spiritually, and mentally than most African American males his age that live in his area of Brooklyn; therefore, I selected him as someone who is living the Islamic principle of "avoiding the traps." I conducted this interview at the Islamic Guidance Center on Atlantic Avenue in Brooklyn, New York in 2009. We began the interview discussing negative personal experiences, and how the discontentment of that life brought him to practicing Islam.

LLEWELLYN COLEMAN (HAJJI NAJI)

It takes some moral fiber to go against the majority. Allah chooses his Muslims. Most of the brothers in this masjid and myself have the same background. And the fact that we all were from the same direction in the *dunya* was that we weren't followers in the *dunya*, we went our own way according to what we believed was just for us. Just like the Prophet Muhammad said that there will be 73 different directions, and all will be mislead except for one.

After doing the street stuff, selling drugs and hanging out, it was time for some spirituality in my life. Christianity didn't look good for me when I was a quote unquote Christian. I always had a problem with Jesus being God and the son of God. So, Allah put me in front of a group of people that were Muslims. I used to drink beer, and I would hide it behind my back when I was around Muslims. I didn't know that Muslims couldn't drink. It was just an aura about them.

The foundation that I got from my parents, that's the key. That was the beginning of my morality which led me to the deen. Support. I don't even think support was grand. There was a lot of envy.

My father is one of the best men that I know. From being a parent and having had relationships I respect him and admire him for his steadfastness. I get strength from just dealing with him. I used to hate to see him coming. He used to discipline me and never explained "why" he disciplined me. I worked the job that he did, and what he did for us, and I understood why. He's a better man than me. He had a lot of reasons to leave. He's been with my mother for over 67 years. I know my mother, and I would've left her (he grins). Sura Nisaa always hit me (a chapter from the Quran that deals with the responsibilities of men to their families).

I had very little trouble with the law because of that situation that I told you about where my mom put me in a certain frame of mind. I had one little B misdemeanor thing when I was 23. I was fortunate enough that Allah blessed me. I was out there in the *dunya* doing all of those things—selling drugs, hanging out, drinking, getting high, and all that. So, he kept all that away from me. And when I did have my scrape (with the law) I wasn't even about that. I was getting out. I was beginning college at 23. Unfortunately that fell on me, but it was an awakening.

Without the *diin* I would never be where I'm at now. On that track that I was on before (he laughs), I don't even know how I made 15 years at Brookdale Hospital—coming to work hung over, sleeping behind my desk. Crossing that line just enough that I get my hands smacked, then I cross back over and stay for a good while until I get underneath the radar. It wasn't exactly 15 years because the last 5 or 6 years I was on the deen. But it (Islam) took me away from that life, having respect for myself and for my family, which I somewhat had that already. Even my mother said when I took my *shahada*, "It doesn't surprise me that you're Muslim, because you were always kind of different in some ways than the rest of my kids." But Alhamdulillah, this is the thing. Without this I couldn't have made it. I had too many bad habits.

Now I'm a director of Marketing. I go to hospitals all over New York City and meet with case managers, social workers, and whoever is in charge of discharging and placing patients in short term or long term. We have an obesity bariatric program where we take patients up to 700 pounds. You might have even seen it air on TLC. I go and I recruit patients for facilities.

It's a Jewish owned facility, but there are a lot of African Americans in healthcare in general. As far as doing my job it's about fifty-fifty (black and white). I went to Hajj 10 days after I started. It was a prerequisite prior to them hiring me. I told them I was already set up for Hajj and that if they were going to hire me that I was going to have to take off a month. So, I worked for a week and went to Hajj the following week.

Overcoming the Trap of Believing that You Can't Succeed Because of Discrimination
You got to be into a position to even have somebody discriminate against you. So, for you to say that I'm not going to go for this job or that job because of discrimination and biases that may cause then you're never going to have an opportunity. I didn't start out doing what I'm doing. I started out in the hospital mopping floors, because I had a family, and I had to support them. So, with that opportunity to be in a situation where there were more opportunities, I took advantage of what was there. I did 5 years of that, I did 4 other departments before I got a marketable skill for myself out of that position, and I went out and sold myself to this facility where I'm at now in terms of better money.

There's people that say I don't want to work in McDonalds, but would you rather have, no food on your table, your kids hungry? You got to start somewhere. So, us, innate, being able to survive in any situation, if you put yourself in it, you're going to be able to come up. You're going to have to be able to accept the opportunities there. If you don't start from the bottom, then you're not going to have a chance to use that natural thing that seems to be a part of our survival. You can go to McDonalds and come out of there and be somebody. They got that whole thing from A to Z, flipping burgers on up. It's just about what your goals are, and if you're capable of taking advantage of the situation that's put in front of you. A lot of people just flip the burgers, get tired, and leave, but I see a lot of guys that own "ten" McDonalds that just started out flipping burgers. That's one of the few companies that made money through this whole recession.

I get paid to sell myself. I'm a salesman. I sell my facility, I sell our services. Why am I able to do that? Because I'm able to deal with different people. I can make some people laugh and smile; you got to know when to hold it, you got to know when to fold it. I've went to facilities and there were white people sitting there, and I come in and they're not open to me. So, instead of me trying to be so on "them", I do my job, I give them the information I have, and I leave. But persistence! I keep going back to that same place until you get to know the people and they open up the door for you. So, those same people that were harsh and closing the door on me in the beginning are the same people that I deal with every day on a working relationship. It's persistence. If they had any problem with me, whatever it was, I didn't let it stop me from doing what I was getting paid to do. That was my job. I had to get paid. So, whatever their hang-ups were, I didn't let that stop me. I just kept coming back until a trust opened up between us.

Avoiding the Trap of Trusting the Media
Once this lady that I was working with, her son was a fireman, they lived in Broad Channel where they had a parade where they (him and other fireman and police officers) had a mockery of this black guy in Jasper, Texas that was dragged with a rope behind a truck and decapitated him.

So that thing had transpired, "unannounced to me." So the mom and I worked together, and some coworkers had brought some flowers to her job for her birthday, but she didn't come. The next day I brought the flowers to her home. The media was outside of her home (about her son's spectacle in the Broad Channel parade). So they took it as if I was celebrating this heinous crime that took place (he laughs). I took a good beaten from that (from friends throughout New York City). The reporters asked me what kind of guy the son was. I told them that I never had a problem with him. Was he a racist? I didn't know. He never appeared that way to me. He was the son of my coworker. I met him, but I didn't know him. I was just delivering her some flowers because she couldn't carry them for her birthday.

My main thing where I really got myself in a problem is that I had a problem with Giuliani. I felt he was a racist and he was doing a lot of things that I didn't agree with. So, they asked me how I felt about him arbitrarily firing the firemen and the police. I told them honestly that I didn't believe, whether right or wrong, that he had the right to arbitrarily fire somebody for that. They were off on their own time, and I didn't understand, him as a mayor, how he could just fire them although they were wrong. Everyone called me a Tom, but I stood up for what I believed in. It could've been me. What if I was in that position? What if Giuliani would just say "I don't like what you said, so you got to leave." So, I spoke on it. Even my dad looked at me kind of harsh (he laughs). What I did learn is that when you see those types of things coming, the thing to say is "no comment." What I said was sliced up. I said a lot more than just that, but that is what they wanted to hear, that's what they had in the paper, and the film clip, what they wanted to hear. They painted me up as though I was agreeing with this guy and that I was happy with this situation (what he did), and I didn't even know what was going on.

Avoiding the Trap of Believing that You Have No Control Over Affairs in Your Life
We sit back and wait for parody, and parody is never going to come. They're never going to "give" you anything. You got to go take it. And that's what this cat on my job (told me). He's Italian, but he works for the Jews. And what happened was I said, "Hey you guys are not paying me enough for my job. And I'm telling you this is the scale of what they're paying marketers now." So, I go at them for a little bit like this. I go on an interview; this business that I'm in is small. It's large, but it's small in terms of everybody knows everybody, and what goes on is heard out there. So, he heard that I went on a few interviews and he brings me into his office, obviously he doesn't want to lose me. He said, "I'm going to tell you something, Lu, these people aren't going to give you their money. You gotta come in, and you gotta 'demand' it." And I got a substantial raise from that, but I'll never forget what he said, "You think these people are just going to give you their money. If you think you're forty thousand dollars underpaid, and you just make a little noise about it, do you think they're just going to give you forty thousand dollars." So, what I had to do was I went on those interviews and showed that I was serious about making some moves. They got wind of it, and they called me in and hooked me up.

Avoiding the Trap of not Accepting and Loving Your Identity
When we don't have somebody on top of our necks (black people) forcing us to do something it doesn't get done. I find this even in the business world that when a black man is working for another black man the owner, being a black man, has higher expectations from his black employees, Like "I'm a brother, you should do this better for me" (he points his finger), and the black employee doesn't feel as though he has to do as much because this is a brother. It should actually be the opposite. It should be that we are both doing the best that we can do to build our thing as black men for each other. But we look to take advantage of that. But we have to be told what we have to do. This one wants to go that way that one wants to go the other.

It's like what I felt about the deen, wearing the Islamic "so called" *sunnah* outfit. Once we get into anything be it Yahweh Ben Yahweh (Hebrew Israelites) or whatever, it seems as though we get into it so deep until we have to take on the identity of that thing, because it's like we don't have an identity. Like the Eastern Parkway thing (Labor Day Parade) the blacks from different countries have two flags. They have the American flag, they may have the Trinidadian flag. We fly with what? Just one flag here. It's like we don't have an identity. And when we get into something, we want to start wearing the turbans, we want to, wear the jalabiyyahs; we want to pray so hard that we don't even think about getting a job which is *haram*. And when we get to start thinking for ourselves without somebody telling us what to do, there's anarchy. And this mosque is a big proof of it.

When I went to Hajj it came to me—I'm not an Arab. And Islam is in your heart, it's the deen. I got a real reality check one time by going to another mosque, and I had on the jalabiyyah, and my jeans, and I'm saying all of these are my brothers (he smiles sarcastically), and they let me know I wasn't one of them. What happened was that my step children were going to that Islamic school, and they did something that they weren't supposed to do. So, I'm speaking to the principle, and he's yelling and screaming, and I'm trying to say look akh (brother) you don't have to talk to me like that, we're all brothers, these are my kids. He said, "These are not your kids!" He was just yelling and screaming. So, the sheikh even approached me and my wife, who worked at the place, kind of harsh. We came into the office and set up a meeting for the next day. So, the next day I came to the meeting in my work clothes, "business clothes", which was a suit and tie. The whole attitude towards me was completely different: "Oh, *'Brother'* Naji", (he extends his hand). I was somebody alright then because I had on a suit and tie.

They made me realize that these clothes are for the elements from where these people come from. It's hot (over there). I don't have to wear any of that to be a Muslim. All I have to do is submit. It showed me that they don't have respect for a black man even in this religion. They saw me as an average black cat that just "wanted" to be a Muslim, that got on a turban. They paid more respect to my suit than they did to me.

When I went to Hajj and saw the house of Abraham, I said to myself that I'm never going to follow any man in this religion, because I have enough. I have the Quran and the *sunnah* of the Prophet Muhammad, and I don't have to wear the jalabiyyahs and the kufis or any of that to say *la ilaha ila llah Muhammad ar Rasuwlallah*. I'm a Muslim: just one who submits (to the will of Allah).

CHAPTER 14

Accept the Oneness

92. *Verily, this (Islam) is your group, one group and I am your Lord! Therefore worship ye Me (alone)!* (al Quran 21:92)

Notice how the oneness of Allah (س) and the oneness of the Muslim nation are emphasized within the same sentence. Accepting the oneness of Allah (س) is the beginning to accepting the oneness of humanity. Although this step is cited last it could have been first.

Islam means submission to *one* God. This belief is inseparable with the implementation of justness. The belief in one God is far greater than superstitions and spookiness. The belief in one God reminds us of our obligations to one another. The person who is not god-fearing does not necessarily owe any loyalty to someone in their absence. However, the person who believes in God knows that no matter how far in the desert he goes, no matter what closet he hides in, he can never escape the sight of God. This belief is like having a little police officer over one's shoulder making sure that he does not deviate from the right course. This belief gives us a greater sense of responsibility towards one another.

Just as God's greatness is indivisible, so is the unique human bond that we have between one another. Accepting the oneness of humanity brings us closer to the obligations that we have towards one another as human beings. Considering ourselves separate and dehumanizing one another only creates social discord and opens the door to counter racism and oppression. Dehumanizing one's self, and believing that you do not have a place in society also creates a hatred and jealousy of others. This eliminates all optimism and makes you a time bomb.

I know that this may be hard to accept, especially for those of us that grew up in the midst of a covert race war. However, this is the same way that El-Hajj Malik El-Shabazz felt until he made his pilgrimage to Mecca and experienced the phenomenon of international brotherhood. This brotherhood does not necessarily constitute things such as intermarrying to symbolically prove one's love for another people; it is far greater. It can mean that I can have my community, you can have yours, yet we can still coexist and exalt one another to excellence.

* * *

People may argue that the concept of the oneness of humanity, and a "genuine" love amongst the different races is impossible; however, I saw this lived out in the life of the last interviewee, "Muhammad Latif." He is a Caucasian American that lives in Valdosta, GA. Valdosta is visibly segregated, where people know their side of the color line and rarely cross it. Muhammad is an exception. He operates a men's clothing store with an Egyptian and an African American.

In his case, his ability to relate to and understand African Americans came from him being marginalized from the rest of society when he lived in Egypt and the Middle East. This takes us back to the first principle of "reeducation" which helps us close the gaps with others through education. This is why all the principles of this book are interrelated and important to "live".

MUHAMMAD LATIF

I was born in Tennessee and lived there until I was six. Then I moved to Egypt with my mom and stepfather. I also lived in Oman. I stayed there for most of my childhood. I lived in Egypt for 4 years and Oman for 5. When I was 15 I came back to the states. Been here ever since. I started practicing Islam when I was 6. They hadn't instilled any Christian teachings. Islam is the first religion that I was exposed to. Once you're Muslim and you understand Islam you can't go back because any other belief system you're going to consider it inferior to Islam. Because you go back from worshipping one creator to worshipping, this, that, or "these".

People talk to you and you don't understand and they don't understand. I can't exactly tell you when I learned Arabic, there just came a time when I realized that I could speak Arabic really well. It was while I was in Egypt. It's a good thing to be different from everybody else, and a bad thing. It's good because you stand out and get attention; people want to talk to you and things like that. The bad part is that not all attention is positive. People may try to single you out of a group and give you some type of hardship for that. When I was in Egypt my schoolmates always considered me an American, so they would call me "Hawaga", which in Egyptian Arabic goes back to when the Caucasian landowners who were called "Hawaga". That was my nickname. It wasn't used offensively, but at the same time it didn't portray who I was, and it wasn't a compliment. It irked me every time I heard it. I had to just let it roll off my shoulders when I heard it.

One thing you have to learn about Middle Eastern countries is that the Islam that you're reading about in the books is not what you're going to see in any Middle Eastern country. You have to make a difference between what's Islam and what's Muslims trying to practice Islam. They may not always do a good job of it. It's a whole country of different types of people. Maybe it's changing now, but before people just assumed that people had knowledge just because they were from the Middle East. You'll go over there and find the people who are right, but you'll also find the people that aren't on the deen. You think you'll go over there and it will be like the books, but it's a normal society that has its pros and cons.

It was definitely a hardship growing up in Egypt, but I wouldn't trade it for anything in the world because it made me who I am today. I have the ability to look at people for who they are, because if you spend some time where people single you out because you're different, then you'll realize how stupid and redundant it is to do that and think that way especially if you're a victim of it. I wasn't any different than any other kid my age. I ate the same food they did, I watched the same TV shows; I was inspired by the same things. And I knew that, maybe they didn't, so now that I hold that it helps define who I am today. Because when I look at people I look at their character. And your character is what is going to make me fall in love with you or distance myself from you, and I realize that it has absolutely nothing to do with race. Allah (س) shielded me from that type of ignorance.

I would say that I'm European, because I really can't connect with America because there are so many different people with different backgrounds that make up this place. I can't feel as though my roots are here. I do realize that my family generations ago occupied this place. If I had a connection with anyplace I would say Europe.

When we say *tawhid al ummah*. It means unity. In all we are the same in essence. Descendants of Adam and Hawaa. When you're hungry I'm hungry; when you're full, I'm full. Then you have *tawhid al ummah*. Then we don't have things like race, selfish desires, ignorance, lack of patience. You would think that the human mind wouldn't waste so much time on silly issues: "Are you from the same place I'm from? Do you follow the same *madhab* I do? And when you go back to the root of the teachings of the prophet you'll see that these things were never an issue.

It's more about finding out what destroys our oneness. And finding out inside ourselves and labeling it and saying this is something we need to get rid of. And once we can do that we can really see true progress.

I'm with the truth, and wherever it takes me I'm going to follow it. If the truth leads me to a bunch of European Caucasians in Bosnia then that's where it leads me. If it leads me to a room full of Malaysians and African Americans, then I'm going to be with the truth no matter where the truth is. If it leads to people that's not of my own race, well, then "boo hoo." I'm going to stick with the truth. And I feel more comfortable around Muslims that understand the deen rather than be with people of my own race that don't understand it. My comfort comes from being around people no matter what their race is; it's the ideas that they carry, how they perceive Allah (س). We have the exact same lifestyles the same ambitions; we know what we want from this life. If you put me in a room full of people with no *aqida*, no *minhaj*, Islam is what brings us together. What's beneath the skin is what attracts us to each other. And that bond is stronger than any bond put there by genetics.

If I no longer look at Rashad (his coworker and close friend) as being a "black" man, and he doesn't look at me as being a white man, I'm Muhammad and he's Rashad, and we deal with each other as "men", that's the start. Most of it comes out of pride. People are so proud of their own

Accept the Oneness

origin that they begin to alienate others. They make other people feel different. But if we overlook all of this and just look at each other as people... I got this from the Prophet's (ﷺ) *sunnah*. According to his *sunnah* you never describe someone by a physical feature, like if someone has a big head, or if someone is black, or white. The only time that you use these descriptions is to literally describe someone who just left, like "you know the black brother who was just here, or the brother with the big forehead." But to call somebody that and let that be there tag this was forbidden by the Rasuwl Allah, you couldn't meet someone and say okay I'm going to make your kunya the "black Man." So, this teaches the Muslim that the Prophet didn't look at people by their physical characteristics, but by the character that they showed. He would name people after something good, *hasan*. He met a man whose name meant rugged and harsh and he changed it to something good. If you take any time to look at someone's ethnicity or physical traits and judge them upon that, you're amongst the ignorant people. You lack intellect.

Definitely When people see me it stands out in their mind, I get stares and things like that (for wearing an Islamic garb), but it depends on your approach. If you're trying to do *dawah* to people, it's best not to shock them as soon as you meet them. But if I'm on my own personal time, at salaatul Jumah, I prefer to dress like this. And if it strikes up a conversation with somebody then *alhamdullilah*, that's an opportunity for me to give *dawah*. If someone is agitated with the way I look then they have a sickness in their heart, and it has nothing to do with me. So, either way it goes, it shouldn't bother me. If someone has that sickness in their heart, they're going to have it whether they see me or not.

If I could change anything, I wouldn't want people to be motivated on solely on selfish desires. That's the one thing that I wish I could change. You see so much of human beings interacting with each other based solely on personal gain. It's constantly being reiterated in the Quran and *hadith* to look out for the *masakin*, the homeless, the orphans. The whole scheme of it all is to not be so worried about yourself. The Prophet said that the *sadaqah* and the *zakaat* purify the heart. This is the same disease as selfishness, so when you put that to the test you know that you can do things for yourself, but if you give it away for nothing but the pleasure of Allah you purify yourself from self desires. I think that this is what is going to bring this country to its knees.

There's a beautiful *hadith* that says, "*La farqa bayna arabiyan wa ijma'iyan ila bi taqwa.*" There's no difference between an Arab and an *agami*, a non-Arab except by their *taqwa*, so the true measure of who someone is based upon their *taqwa* (fear of God).

* * *

Muhammad lives the life that Malcolm X saw when he visited Mecca. In *The Autobiography of Malcolm X* he is quoted by Alex Haley as saying:

> Back at the Frankfurt airport, we took a United Arab Airlines plane on to Cairo. Throngs of people, obviously Muslims from everywhere, bound on the pilgrimage, were hugging and embracing. They were of all complexions, the whole atmosphere was of warmth and of friendliness. The feeling hit me that there really wasn't any color problem here. The effect was though I had just stepped out of prison.[1]

Malcolm then met an Egyptian born Saudi citizen named Abdul Rahman Azzam, an international statesman and one of the closest advisors of Prince Faisal, the ruler of Saudi Arabia, who followed Malcolm X very closely. Malcolm X read his book called the *Eternal Message of* Muhammad. Malcolm said:

> I will never forget the dinner at the Azzam home. I quote my notebook again: "I couldn't say in my mind that these were 'white' men. Why, the men acted as if they were brothers of mine; the elder Dr. Azzam as if he were my father. His fatherly, scholarly speech. I felt like he was my father. He was, you could tell, a highly skilled diplomat, with a broad range of mind. His knowledge was so worldly. He was as current on world affairs as some people are to what's going on in their living room.
>
> The more we talked, the more his vast reservoir of knowledge and its variety seemed unlimited. He spoke of the racial lineage of the descendants of Muhammad the Prophet, and he showed how they were both black and white. He also pointed out how colors, the complexities

of color, and the problems of color which exist in the Muslim world has been influenced by the West. He said that if one encountered any differences based on attitude toward color, this directly reflected the degree of Western influence.²

Finally, Malcolm sent a letter to his loyal assistants at his newly founded Mosque, Inc. in Harlem. The letter was duplicated and then distributed to the press. As myself, Malcolm experienced the centuries old concept of *international brotherhood* which he describes clearly in his letter:

> Never have I witnessed such sincere hospitality and the overwhelming spirit of true brotherhood as is practiced by people of all colors and races here in this Ancient Holy Land, the home of Abraham, Muhammad, and all the other prophets of the Holy Scriptures. For the past week, I have been utterly speechless and spellbound by the graciousness I see displayed all around me by people of all colors.
>
> I have been blessed to visit the Holy City of Mecca. I have made my seven circuits around the ka'ba, led by a young Mutawaf named Muhammad. I drank water from the well of Zam Zam. I ran seven times back and forth between the hills of Mt. Al Safa and Al Marwah. I have prayed in the ancient city of Mina, and I have prayed on Mt. Arafat.
>
> There were tens of thousands of pilgrims, from all over the world. They were of all colors, from blue-eyed blonds to black-skinned Africans. But we were all participating in the same ritual, displaying a spirit of unity and brotherhood that my experiences in America had led me to believe never could exist between the white and the non-white.
>
> America needs to understand Islam, because this is the one religion that erases from society the race problem. Throughout my travels in the Muslim world, I have met, talked to, and even eaten with people who in America would have been considered 'white'—but the 'white' attitude was removed from their minds by the religion of Islam. I have never before seen sincere and true brotherhood practiced by all colors together, irrespective of their color.
>
> You may be shocked by these words coming from me. But *on this* pilgrimage, what I have seen, and experienced, has forced me to rearrange much of my thought-patterns previously held, and to toss aside some

of my previous conclusions. This was not too difficult for me despite my firm convictions, I have been always a man who tries to face facts, and to accept the reality of life as new experience and new knowledge unfolds it. I have always kept an open mind, which is necessary to the flexibility that must go hand in hand with every form of intelligent search for truth.

During the past eleven days here in the Muslim world, I have eaten from the same plate, drunk from the same glass, and slept in the same bed (or on the same rug)—while praying to the same God—with fellow Muslims, whose eyes were the bluest of blue, whose hair was the blondest of blond, and whose skin was the whitest of 'white', Muslims, I felt the same sincerity that I felt among the black African Muslims of Nigeria, Sudan, and Ghana.

We were truly all the same (brothers)—because their belief in one God had removed the 'white' from their minds, the white from their behavior, and the 'white' from their attitude.

I could see from this, that perhaps if white Americans could accept the Oneness of God, then perhaps, too, they could accept in reality the Oneness of Man-and cease to Measure, and hinder, and harm others in terms of the 'differences' in color.

With racism plaguing America like an incurable cancer, the so-called 'Christian' White American heart should be more receptive to a proven solution to such a destructive problem. Perhaps it could be in time to save America from imminent disaster—the same destruction brought upon Germany by racism that eventually destroyed the Germans themselves.

Each hour here in the Holy Land enables me to have greater spiritual insights into what is happening in America between black and white. The American Negro can never be blamed for his racial animosities—he is only reacting to four hundred years of the conscious racism of the American Whites. But as racism leads America up the suicide path, I do believe, from the experiences that I have had with them, that the whites of the younger generation, in the colleges and universities, will see the hand writing on the wall and many of them will turn to the spiritual path of truth—the only way left for America to ward off the disaster that racism inevitably must lead to.

Never have I been so highly honored. Never have I been made to feel more humble and unworthy. Who would believe the blessings that have been heaped upon an *American Negro?* A few nights ago, a man who would be called a 'white' man, a United Nations diplomat, an ambassador, a companion of kings, gave me his hotel suite, his bed. By this man, His Excellency Prince Faisal, who rules the Holy Land, was made aware of my presence here in Jeddah. The very next morning, Prince Faisal's son, in person, informed me that by the will and decree of his esteemed father, I was to be a state Guest.

Hajj Court. His Holiness gave me two books on Islam, with his personal seal and autograph, and he told me that he prayed that I would be a successful preacher of Islam in America. A car, a driver, and a guide, have been placed at my disposal, making it possible for me to travel about this Holy Land almost at will. The government provides air-conditioned quarters and servants in each city that I visit. Never would I have even thought of dreaming that I would ever be a recipient of such honors-honors that in America would be bestowed upon a king—not a Negro.

All praise due to Allah, the Lord of all the Worlds.

    Sincerely,
    El Hajj Malik El-Shabbaz (Malcolm X)[3]

INDEX

'abd, 92, 93
Abdul Alim Musa, 124, 125, 126
Abner Louimer, 62
Abolish Slavery, 89
abolitionist, 9, 17, 22
Abraham Lincoln, 20
Abraham's dream, 3
Abu Lahab, 12
Adolf Hitler, 79
Africa, 8, 9, 25, 31, 34, 71, 81, 86, 87, 91, 93, 94, 95, 96, 99, 133
African American culture, 36
African Americans, 20, 21, 26, 33, 34, 38, 42, 43, 46, 48, 49, 53, 57, 58, 59, 62, 63, 66, 84, 99, 100, 101, 102, 104, 111, 112, 119, 124, 132, 133, 142, 146, 159, 166, 169
African ancestry, 7, 92
African descent, 20, 28, 40, 61, 105, 106, 133, 143
Africans, 8, 20, 45, 87, 94, 99, 107, 115, 141, 172
ahadith, 86, 93
al-Mansur, 105
Amadou Diallo, 61, 62
America, 18, 19, 20, 21, 22, 23, 24, 25, 26, 31, 32, 33, 34, 35, 36, 39, 41, 42, 45, 54, 58, 59, 60, 65, 66, 81, 91, 92, 96, 99, 102, 115, 119, 124, 126, 132, 137, 139, 143, 144, 149, 168, 172, 173, 174
American, 9, 19, 20, 21, 22, 25, 26, 27, 28, 30, 31, 34, 36, 37, 42, 43, 46, 48, 52, 53, 57, 58, 59, 60, 61, 62, 63, 71, 73, 83, 94, 95, 99, 100, 102, 106, 111, 112, 113, 114, 115, 116, 119, 121, 123, 125, 132, 133, 138, 139, 140, 143, 145, 147, 149, 157, 163, 166, 167, 173, 174
Anwar al-Sadat, 106
Arab, 7, 13, 14, 86, 90, 91, 92, 94, 97, 98, 102, 105, 106, 113, 115, 118, 132, 141, 151, 163, 170, 171
attributes of God, 9
Ayatollah Ruhullah Khomeini, 99
Ba'th Party, 97, 98

173

banking institutions, 79
Bible, 1
Bilal, 105
black, 8, 20, 22, 23, 25, 29, 30, 31, 32, 34, 35, 36, 37, 38, 39, 42, 43, 45, 49, 51, 54, 57, 58, 59, 60, 92, 93, 94, 95, 99, 102, 104, 105, 106, 107, 113, 114, 115, 119, 133, 136, 138, 139, 140, 141, 146, 147, 149, 151, 153, 159, 161, 162, 164, 169, 171, 172, 173
Black Nationalism
nationalism, 99, 102, 103
blacks, 8, 20, 22, 31, 32, 33, 45, 53, 58, 59, 92, 94, 96, 104, 119, 140, 143, 163
bloodlines, 6, 11, 12
Blue Eye Fallacy, 103
Booker T. Washington, 99
bridging the gaps, 111
Canaan, 3, 7, 8, 10, 13, 19, 22
casinos, 83, 84
Christian, 18, 20, 21, 22, 24, 26, 27, 28, 31, 33, 44, 83, 92, 98, 99, 100, 101, 102, 103, 107, 158, 167, 173
Christianity, 1, 25, 28, 44, 99, 103, 121, 158
Christianization, 23, 24, 25, 26, 85, 100
Christians, 1, 15, 16, 17, 21, 25, 26, 28, 93, 99, 101, 102
Civil Rights, 29, 101
cocaine, 35, 48, 51, 52, 53
Collin Powell, 73

constitution, 19
Cotton Mather, 24
Covenant, 5, 8, 10, 19, 20, 33
crack, 35, 48, 51, 52, 53
Crack, 48, 50, 51, 52, 55, 56
crime, 26, 31, 32, 35, 36, 38, 45, 46, 60, 61, 65, 66, 68, 70, 71, 73, 75, 84, 124, 144, 156, 161
criminal justice system, 48
criminalization, 36, 85
Crown Heights riot, 61
culture, 18, 24, 29, 36, 38, 39, 59, 74, 75, 98, 107, 111, 115, 117, 143, 150, 151
cursed, 8, 9, 17, 104
Cursed, 3, 8
curses, 7, 17, 28
Darfur, 94, 95, 114
David Dinkins, 59
debt, 79, 80, 81, 82, 83, 85, 124
discrimination, 17, 26, 27, 29, 32, 42, 49, 62, 104, 117, 159
Donald Trump, 74, 144
drug trade, 35, 49, 51, 52
drugs, 35, 48, 49, 52, 53, 57, 72, 75, 119, 130, 154, 158
economic barriers, 123
Economic Jihad, 110, 122
Edict of Expulsion, 83
Egypt, 5, 8, 91, 96, 105, 106, 112, 115, 116, 119, 167, 168
empathy, 112
entertainment world, 38, 40, 69
equality, 14, 16, 20, 27, 78, 87, 88, 89, 91, 99, 101, 104
Ethiopians, 8

ethnicity, 6, 9, 10, 11, 14, 24, 105, 170
Euphrates, 5
Eurasian slaves, 91
Europe, 25, 87, 91, 93, 96, 107, 139, 168
family relations, 12
family structure, 64, 66, 68, 71, 74, 143
family ties, 12, 142, 145
felony, 40, 45, 49, 65
Felony disenfranchisement, 45
fire department, 146, 148
first black fireman, 147
forgiveness, 11, 12, 14
Frederick Douglas' speech, 22
Frederick Douglass, 9
freedom, 75, 76, 96, 99, 101, 105, 143
gambling, 83, 84
geographical location, 2, 109
George Allen, 30, 31
Giuliani, 60, 61, 62, 63, 161
God, 1, 2, 3, 4, 5, 6, 7, 8, 9, 10, 11, 12, 13, 14, 15, 16, 17, 19, 20, 21, 22, 23, 25, 28, 30, 70, 76, 77, 78, 82, 88, 89, 90, 91, 93, 101, 102, 103, 104, 107, 129, 142, 156, 157, 158, 165, 166, 173
Greenwood, 58
Hagar, 5
Ham, 7, 8, 9, 20, 22, 28, 33, 63
Ham's descendants, 7, 8
Harlem, 8, 54, 59, 60, 132, 172
Hebrews, 2, 8, 9, 10, 11, 12, 103

Hollywood, 69, 137
Holocaust, 16
Identity, 150, 162
Imam Ja'far as-Saadiq, 105
Imam Musa al-Kaazim, 105
incarcerated, 33, 34, 48, 53
incarceration, 34, 45, 46, 65, 75
Indians, 21, 22, 132, 137, 141
Individual racism, 29
injustices, 17, 18, 21, 23, 26, 27, 28, 62, 66, 99, 120
inmates, 34, 57, 78
institutional racism, 29, 32, 40, 41, 46, 57, 64
interest, 38, 39, 77, 78, 79, 80, 81, 82, 84, 85, 103, 124, 126, 133
international brotherhood, 166, 172
Iraq, 3, 70, 96, 98, 106, 148
Isaac, 2, 5, 7, 11, 82
Ishmael, 2, 5, 7, 45
Islam, 1, 2, 6, 7, 9, 12, 13, 14, 15, 16, 17, 48, 63, 71, 72, 74, 78, 84, 86, 87, 88, 90, 91, 92, 93, 97, 98, 100, 101, 102, 103, 105, 107, 114, 115, 116, 118, 119, 120, 121, 124, 125, 127, 128, 131, 134, 145, 148, 150, 157, 159, 163, 165, 167, 169, 172, 174
Israel, 3, 9, 13, 83, 106
Israelites, 2, 7, 9, 10, 11, 13, 19, 22, 82, 103, 140, 163
jail, 30, 34, 153
Jamal 'Abdun-Nasser, 92
Janjaweed militia, 94
Japheth, 7, 8, 20, 28

Jeffrey Rodriguez, 72
Jesus, 1, 8, 13, 22, 101, 102, 158
Jews, 1, 17, 40, 44, 61, 79, 82, 83, 126, 162
jihad, 83, 88, 128
Jim Crow laws, 16, 29, 99
Judaism, 1, 82, 126
Judeo-Christian, 2, 8, 18, 39, 63, 92, 93, 99, 102, 107
justice, 2, 14, 28, 34, 40, 46, 57, 62, 68, 87, 88, 89, 101, 126, 143
justness of Allah, 2
Kemal Ataturk, 96, 97
Ku Klux Klan, 26, 103
Kyle Burton, 43, 145, 146, 147
law, 16, 20, 27, 28, 33, 36, 37, 44, 46, 53, 58, 61, 63, 66, 71, 72, 73, 79, 86, 96, 97, 101, 103, 143, 147, 158
Leadership, 105, 110, 131, 133
legislative obstacles, 58
lineage, 2, 5, 6, 7, 9, 10, 12, 171
Llewellyn Coleman, 157
Malcolm X, 171, 174
Mamluks, 91
mankind, 1, 2, 10, 13, 14, 16, 17, 126
martyrdom of Imam Hussein, 112
Mason T. Lowance, 22, 23
Master Fard Muhammad, 101
Mecca, 1, 59, 63, 89, 166, 171, 172
media, 40, 42, 52, 75, 76, 94, 101, 114, 115, 116, 143, 161
messenger, 1
Michel 'Aflaq, 96

Mike Tyson, 73
Minister Louis Farrakhan, 102, 111
minorities, 26, 29, 30, 32, 33, 34, 35, 37, 38, 39, 43, 49, 62
minority communities, 35, 49, 83, 84
mizan, 14, 87
Moorish Americans, 139
Moors, 49, 107, 139
Muhammad, 1, 6, 7, 12, 13, 48, 63, 89, 90, 91, 97, 98, 99, 100, 101, 102, 103, 104, 105, 107, 146, 158, 164, 166, 167, 169, 171, 172
Muhammad Reza Shah, 98
murder rate, 71
Muslim countries, 41, 103
Muslims, 1
Nation of Islam, 101, 125
New Testament, 23
Noah, 7, 103
NYPD, 61, 62
Obama, 48, 82, 131
Old Testament, 23
oppressed, 14, 15, 16, 23, 26, 39, 63, 88, 100, 124, 134, 141, 146, 155
oppression, 8, 15, 17, 22, 23, 28, 29, 40, 48, 65, 76, 77, 82, 85, 86, 87, 88, 102, 103, 122, 123, 134, 144, 146, 152, 166
oppressive elements, 45, 75, 85
oppressors, 16, 17, 22, 23, 26, 99, 102
Ottoman Empire, 91, 96, 107
Palestinians, 44, 111

Persia to Iran, 93, 98
Persians, 8, 93, 98
Pharaoh, 106, 107, 110, 120
plantations, 24
policies, 29, 30, 44, 45, 57, 62, 111
prejudices, 12, 119, 120, 149
prison, 34, 35, 48, 53, 63, 65, 72, 75, 131, 143, 153, 171
prophecy, 9
Quran, 1, 2, 5, 6, 7, 9, 10, 11, 12, 13, 14, 15, 16, 17, 48, 63, 69, 70, 74, 77, 78, 82, 85, 86, 87, 88, 89, 90, 91, 93, 100, 101, 103, 104, 107, 109, 110, 111, 120, 121, 122, 126, 129, 136, 141, 142, 156, 157, 158, 164, 165, 170
race, 2, 9, 10, 16, 17, 19, 20, 21, 25, 26, 27, 30, 40, 43, 58, 59, 66, 92, 95, 98, 103, 104, 105, 107, 109, 113, 129, 130, 137, 141, 166, 168, 169, 172
races, 7, 8, 20, 30, 37, 91, 103, 166, 172
racial superiority, 11, 21
racism, 21, 22, 23, 29, 34, 41, 42, 43, 48, 57, 62, 63, 64, 85, 86, 94, 97, 102, 112, 121, 123, 133, 144, 146, 147, 148, 149, 152, 166, 173
Racism, 29, 34, 43, 114
Rdwon Raffay, 114
Reeducation, 110, 118, 150
retaliation, 14
revelation, 1, 2
Rick Ruben, 40

rights, 10, 11, 14, 15, 16, 27, 29, 65, 101, 131
rioting, 61
Rudolf Giuliani, 60, 61
Sammy Young Jr., 26
Sarah, 3, 5
segregation, 11, 16, 23, 26, 29, 30, 46, 58, 99, 103
Seljuks, 91
servant
servants, 8, 12, 82, 93, 107
Shaikh Saed Ali Kulayni, 132
Shem, 7, 8, 20
Shia, 132, 133
Sioux, 137
slave, 5, 22, 24, 25, 33, 34, 66, 67, 79, 88, 89, 90, 92, 93, 94, 99, 105, 107, 115, 124, 131
slavery, 8, 9, 20, 22, 23, 24, 25, 26, 29, 32, 33, 34, 36, 45, 46, 59, 66, 85, 89, 91, 92, 94, 152
slaves, 7, 25, 42, 49, 66, 89, 90, 91, 92, 93
social acceptance, 37, 38
socio-economic, 2, 49, 94, 136, 138, 145
south, 9, 30, 36, 95, 114, 116, 143
stealth, 29, 40, 41, 64
stereotype
stereotypes, 52, 151, 152
Student Non-Violent Coordinating Committee, 26
submissiveness, 16
Sudan, 93, 95, 114, 115, 173
Sudan People's Liberation Army (SPLA), 95

sunnah, 140, 163, 164, 169
Sunnah, 87
Sunni, 98, 114, 132, 133
superior, 9, 17, 20, 21, 98, 103
The Federal Communications Committee, 39
The Fresh Prince of Bellaire, 37
The Obama Deception, 82
The Tulsa Race Riot of 1921, 58
Thirteenth Amendment, 32, 33
Thomas Jefferson's first Inaugural Address, 19
Time Magazine, 27
Torah, 1, 6
Trap, 159, 161, 162
traps, 83, 153, 156, 157
Tuskegee, 26, 27
Umar bin Khattaab, 105
United States, 20, 26, 32, 35, 41, 42, 43, 46, 48, 49, 58, 59, 63, 70, 71, 75, 82, 83, 101, 106, 114, 116, 128, 138
war on drugs, 35, 52
Waseem Akhtar, 116, 119, 144
white, 9, 20, 21, 26, 28, 30, 31, 32, 33, 34, 35, 36, 39, 43, 44, 48, 53, 57, 58, 59, 94, 98, 101, 102, 104, 112, 115, 116, 119, 121, 127, 136, 138, 141, 146, 147, 148, 152, 159, 160, 169, 171, 172, 173, 174
Willie Lynch, 66, 68, 75
Ya'qub Ibn Yusuf, 105
zihaar, 90, 91
Zionists, 40, 82, 126

NOTES

1 End Notes

Preface
1. Barack Obama, *2004 Democratic National Convention Keynote Address,* delivered 27 July 2004, Fleet Center, Boston.

Chapter 1 / The Bible and The Quran: pillars of the World
1. G. Laurie, ed., *New Believers Bible* (Wheatley: Tyndale House P, 1996).
2. J.P. Boyd, A.M., *The Practical Bible Dictionary and Concordance,* (Uhrichsville: Barbour, 1952).
3. H. Greeley, *Two Hours with Brigham Young,* interview, Salt Lake City, 1859, Microsoft Encarta Reference, 2004.
4. F. Douglass, *Narrative of the Life of Frederick Douglass, n American Slave* (Boston: Anti-Slavery Society, 1845), p.17
5. M.N. Ar-Rifa'i, *Tafsir Ibn Kathir* (London: Al Firdous Ltd., 1998), p.184.
6. Ibid. p.184.

Chapter 2 / Racist Blueprint
1. C. B. Carson, *The Beginning of the Republic* 1775-1825 (Wadley: American Textbook Committee, 1984), p.86.
2. M. I Lowance, *Against Slavery: An Abolitionist Reader* (New York: Penguin, 2000), p. 223.

Chapter 3 / You Better Recognize: the stealth of institutional racism.
1. http://www.blogdenovo.org/archives/1874.html

2. http://www.time.com/time/magazinearticle/0,9171,984134,00.html.
3. I interviewed Kyle Burton personally on Tuesday, July 28, 2009 at his home in Brooklyn, New York.
4. The World, *Palestinians Counter Sharon with Higher Education, The New Federalist*, Volume XVIII, August 9, 2004.
5. Ibid.
6. Waler Matthews Grant, *Special Project-The Collateral Consequences of a Criminal Conviction,* 23 Vand.
L. Rev. 929, 941 (1970).
7. http://strongsnumbers.com/greek/3498.html.
8. Mark E. Thompson, *Don't do the Crime If You Ever Intend to Vote Again*, 33 Seton Hall L. Rev. 167, 175 (2002).
9. The Sentencing Project, Felony Disenfranchisement Laws in the United States 1 (2005), http://sentencingproject.org/pdfs/1046.pdf; *see also* Demos-USA, Restoring Voting Rights to Citizens with Felony Convictions 1 (2003), *at* http://www.demos.org/page26.cfm.
10. *See* The Sentencing Project, *supra* note 115, at 1; *see also* Calmore, *supra* note 52, at 1274 ("Of [the] total, 1.5 million, or 37.5 percent, are African Americans.").
11. This figure includes those who consider themselves a combination of black and another race. U.S. Census Bureau, Race Alone or in Combination: 2000 (2000), *available at* American Fact Finder, http://factfinder.census.gov/servlet/SAFFFactsCharIteration?_submenuId=factsheet_2&_sse=on (select "Black alone or in combination with one or more other races").
12. http://en.wikipedia.org/wiki/Criminology
13. http://www.shadowofmeth.com/statistics.html
14. http://www.nytimes.com/2006/10/24/world/americas/24iht-dems.3272493.html?_r=1
15. http://WWW.salon.com/news/feature/1999/10/18/cocaine
16. http://WWW.papillonsartpalace.com/cocaine.html
17. USSC, *Report to Congress: Cocaine and Federal Sentencing Policy*, May 2007, p. 36.
18. Ibid., p. 32.
19. Ibid., p. 33.
20. Ibid., p. 68.

21. Testimony of Deborah A. Frank, M.D. before the United States Sentencing Commission, February 21, 2002.
22. Dorothy K. Hatsukami, and Marian W. Fischman, "Crack Cocaine and Cocaine Hydrochloride: Are the Differences Myth or Reality?" *Journal of the American Medical Association*, November 20, 1996.
23. Testimony of Charles Schuster before the Subcommittee on Crime and Drugs of the Senate Judiciary Committee, May 22, 2002.
24. Testimony of Commissioner John R. Steer before the Subcommittee on Criminal Justice, Drug Policy and Human Resources, May 11, 2000.
25. *Report to Congress: Cocaine and Federal Sentencing Policy*, May 2002 p. 45, Figure 10.
26. Ibid., p. 100.
27. USSC, *Fifteen Years of Guidelines Sentencing* (Nov. 2004), p. 122.
28. Bureau of Justice Statistics [BJS], *Compendium of Federal Justice Statistics, 1994* (Washington, DC: March 1998) Table 6.11, p. 85 and BJS, *Compendium of Federal Justice Statistics, 2003* (Washington, DC: Oct. 2004) Table 7.16, p. 112.
29. *Compendium of Federal Statistics, 2003* (Oct. 2005), Table 7.16, p. 112.
30. USSC, *Fifteen Years of Guidelines Sentencing* (Nov. 2004), p. 132.
31. http://ezfame.com/tag/molestation-statistics/
32. httpwww.justice.govusaoohsPressPSC%20Powerpoint%20hunter.pdf
33. http://www.drugpolicy.org/library/factsheets/barriers/
34. Up From the Ashes" Tulsa World. March 8, 1993.http://docs.newbank.com/s/InfoWeb/aggdocs/AWNB/OEB547CF5FCFC6FA/0F3172437331D383
35. Madigan, Tim. *The Burning: Massacre, Destruction, and the Tulsa Race Riot of 1921,* New York: St Martin's Press (2001) at pp. 4, 131-132, 144, 159, 164, 249. ISBN 0-312-27283-9.
36. White, Walter F. "The Eruption of Tulsa", *The Nation*
37. Hannibal B. Johnson, Black Wall Street: From Riot to Renaissance in Tulsa's Historic Greenwood District. Austin, TX. 1998.
37. Cheers, D. Michael. "Mayor of 'The Big Apple': 'nice guy' image helps David N. Dinkins in building multi-ethnic, multiracial coalition-New York City", *Ebony* (magazine), Gebruary 1990. Accessed September 4, 2008.

38. Wayne Barrett (2001-06-25). "Giuliani's Legacy: Taking Credit For Things He Didn't Do". *Gotham Gazette.* http://www.gothamgazette.com/commentary/91.barrett.shtml. Retrieved 2007-11-15. (Highly suggested reading for those that want deeper insight to the truths of institutional racism).
39. Patrick A. Langan; Matthew R. Durose (December 2003). "The Remarkable Drop in Crime in New York City" (PDF). International Conference on Crime. http://samoa.istai.it/Eventi/sicurezza/relazioni/Langan_rel.pdg. Retrieved 2007-11-15. "According to NYPD statistics, crime in New York City took a downturn starting around 1990 that continued for many years, shattering all the city's old records for consecutive-year declines in crime rates."
40. "Political Memo: Another Look at the Dinkins Administration, and Not by Giuliani, by Michael Powell, *The New York Times*, October 25, 2009 (p. A19 of Oct. 26, 2009 NY ed.). Retrieved Oct. 26, 2009.
41. Shapiro, Edward S. (2006). *Crown height: Blacks, Jew, and the 1991 Brooklyn Riot.* Waltham, Massachusetts: Brandeis University Press, University Press of New England, http://books. Googl.com/books?id=StQXz-C1GuUC. Retrieved 2007-10-20
42. Mintz, Jerome R. (1992). *Hasidic People: A Place in the New World.* Harvard University Press. pp. 334–335. ISBN 0674381157. http://books.google.com/books?id=uEP5KNUAFh0C. Retrieved 2007-10-20.
43. Shapiro, Edward S. (2006). *Crown Heights: Blacks, Jews, and the 1991 Brooklyn riot.*
Waltham, Massachusetts: Brandeis University Press, University Press of New England. http://books.google.com /books?id=StQXz-C1GuUC. Retrieved 2007-10-20
44. Cohen, D. N. Crown Heights Jews feel vindicated by report. Jewish Tribune (Rockland County, NY), July 23-29, 1993.)
45. *Daily News*, July 1, 1993.
46. The New York Times February 15, 1999, Monday, Late Edition - Final SECTION: Section A; Page 1; Column 4; Metropolitan Desk LENGTH: 1910 words HEADLINE: Success of Elite Police Unit Exacts a Toll on the Streets BYLINE: By DAVID KOCIENIEWSKI

47. Hinojosa, M. (1997.) "NYC officer arrested in alleged sexual attack on suspect". *CNN.com*. Retrieved December 6, 2006
48. http://www.nytimes.com/2006/04/03/nyregion/03blacks.html?pagewanted=print

Chapter 4 / The Destruction of Family
1. http://www.marriagedebate.com/pdf/imapp.crimefamstructure.pdf (September 21, 2005 www.imapp.org)
2. Warren Farrell, (The Myth of Male Power: Why Men Are the Disposable Sex (London: Fourth Estate, 1994),
3. http://en.wikipedia.org/wiki/List_of_countries_by_intentional_homicide_rate
4. http://www.mapsofworld.com/world-top-ten/countries-with-highest-reported-crime-rates.html
5. http://en.wikipedia.org/wiki/Community_Service_Society_of_NewYork
6. http://en.wikipedia.org/wiki/List_of_countries_by_intentional_homicide_rate
7. Letter from Jeffrey Rodriguez, State Correctional Institution at Smithfield (Huntingdon, PA), May 10, 2010.
8. Toback, James, *Tyson,* Sony Pictures Classics, 2009.
9. Trump, Donald, with Charles Leerhsen, *Trump: The Art of Survival,* (New York: Warner Books, 1991) p.49.

Chapter 5 / Usury, and the Bait to Success
1. http://www.hitler.org/writings/Mein_Kampf/mkv1ch08.html (Volume I, Chapter III).
2. Ibid.,,
3. http://members.fortunecity.com/dperkins1/tyranny_of_interest *The Tyranny of Interest* 4/23/1998
4. Robinson, Randal, *The Debt: What America Owes to Blacks,* (New York, Penguin, 2000), p.184.
5. http://www.terry.uga.edu~dmustardcasinos.pdf
6. Thompson, William N., *Gambling in America: an encyclopedia of histories, issues, and society* (Santa Barbara, ABC-CLIO, Inc., 2001) p.87

Chapter 6 / The Quran Verses Islamic Society: separating the two

1. J. S. Trimingham, "Islam in Africa," in *Africa a Handbook to the Continent,* ed. Colin Legum, (New York: Praeger, 1966), p. 475.
2. B. Lewis, *Islam in History,* (Peru: Open Court, 1993), p.205.
3. Ibid. p. 253.
4. Ibid.
5. C. Muhammad, "Darfur: Seeking the Truth," *The Final Call,* August 31, 2004, p.3.
6. Ibid.
7. Ibid, p.14.
8. F. Douglass, "West India Emancipation Speech", Canandaigua, New York, Lowance, ed., *Against Slavery: An Abolitionist Reader.*
9. *Muhammad Speaks,* July 13, 1973, second to last page.
10. L. Farrakhan, *The Million Family March,* (FCI Broadcasting, 734 W. 79th Street, Chicago, Illinois 60620: www.finalcal.com).
11. T. Muhammad, *Chronology of the Nation of Islam,* (Chicago: Steal Away creations, 1996), pp. 2, 20, 37.
12. Muslim, *Sahih Muslim,* Trans. A. H. Siddiqi, ahadith 4523-33.
13. B. Lewis. p. 252.
14. Ibid. chap. 29
15. H. Mohamed, *A review of Autumn of Fury: The Assassination of Sadat* by Mohamed Hekal, Random House, from *The New York Review of Books,* 31 May 1984.
16. Ibid.
17. Muslim. 4523-33

www.ingramcontent.com/pod-product-compliance
Lightning Source LLC
LaVergne TN
LVHW051557070426
835507LV00021B/2618